Celtic Wisdom and Contemporary living

Celtic Wisdom and Contemporary living

Phyllida Anam-Áire

© Phyllida Anam-Áire 2007

First published by Findhorn Press in 2007

ISBN 978-1-84409-113-3

British Library Cataloguing-in-Publication Data.
A catalogue record for this book is available
from the British Library.

Edited by Magaer Lennox
Cover design by Damian Keenan
Interior design by Damian Keenan

Printed and bound by WS Bookwell, Finland

Published by
Findhorn Press
305a The Park, Findhorn
Forres IV36 3TE
Scotland, UK

Telephone
+44-1309-690582
Fax
+44-1309-690036

info@findhornpress.com
www.findhornpress.com

Contents

Contents

Contents

Acknowledgements

Deep appreciation to Hannah Cunningham, for her consistent belief in the ancient wisdom, for embodying it. This is the greatest teaching. Your facilitating at workshops, your presentations at conferences, your healing, soulful presence are all part of your passion as a true Celtic woman. Maybe one day my eyes will see the world as you see it with such vastness and consciousness.

Also thanks to Findhorn Press, and especially to Sabine... *Eine schoene Frau. Herzlichen Dank.* Thanks to Barbara Faro for her nudging and her love, and to Sarah Arivanna Trevelyan for her companionship and devotion to the subject. To all my dear people in Germany, and Findhorn Community. Deep appreciation to my ancestors, and to my own parents who were just perfect for me this time round. Thanks to Richard and Anthea, my two great adult children, and to their father, Tom, for all we share together, and for your belief in me. My sister Mary has been encouraging me to tell the stories and let you, my wider family share them. *Tá grá agam duit a Mháire* I am deeply grateful, and I love you all.

FOREWORD

We live in a modern world, heavily influenced by thought, and technological skills, which have brought us to the point of thinking it is unnecessary to have the powers of the universe within us. Somehow, we have lost, or forgotten, the inner psychic world in its relation to the natural world. We have so often failed to maintain communion with the deeper powers, with the birds that soar, the winds that howl their presence, the mountains that hold the stories of the past, the flowers that share their bounty of colour and fragrance. Where is the validation in us these days, from the ritual integration with the liturgy of the seasons, and the turning of the days, from day to night, and back again. These transitions we once knew as sacred. No longer do we honour the alliance we once knew, and the teacher that held the wisdom for our lives. No longer do we celebrate all of life, or accept sickness and death as part of the creative journey with a meaningful interpretation.

We have, in essence, trivialized our existence by losing our sense of soul. Without the assistance of soul we cannot stand in our power during crisis. We do not know where our power point is. The world we have created, both inside and out, can take us no further, and we need to return again, be awakened, and reawakened to our soul's calling.

Globally, and as individuals, we have become addicted to growth through struggle, and are frequently drawn to living out the belief that 'all life is suffering'. This is not what soul wants for, and from us. When we live from soul, there will be no suffering for we are shown how to detach from pain, once we have fully embraced it. Suffering is our scared earth-mind's attachment to pain. Today's psychology also reinforces the tradition of growth through struggle, for it too has lost connection with soul. The false belief is that pain is a necessary stimulus to growth rather than the last ditch attempt to get our attention, when all else has failed. Yet, there is an alternative to the ancient path of the warrior; the path of fear, struggle, and conflict is not our only option. Embracing Celtic Consciousness will take you on an exciting inner journey where your soul will sing its love song and whisper your story into life.

As you enliven the pages with your own mystery you will find your consciousness expanding, and will discover your internal power, your inner authority, your power centre. A cautionary word is that you must live the experience of Celtic Consciousness. No amount of reading will change anything. You must risk life, relationships, being foolish, being misunderstood, saying no. And you must also risk experiencing the joy of giving and receiving love, seeing in a new dimension, integrating all of yourself, and calling back your projections. This journey will take you deeply into life, into yourself, and into responsibility and commitment. If you dare to live the life you came to Earth for, then read on.

I have learned the true value of living Celtic Consciousness as I live my life with advanced cancer; for my awakened soul has taught me the richness of dying daily and living fully.

Finally, as you journey, a new beauty will be revealed, whereby, all reflection and its expression will be a kind of poetry. You will be both the poet and the poem. When we integrate the secular with the holy, power thrusts through all things. New worlds await you, as they have for me. I recommend you approach this sacred work with an open heart, excitement, and expectation in preparation for the birthing of a new soul song.

Hannah Cunningham
28 January 2006

Dedication

I dedicate this book to all of us who daily dare to rise above our earth-mind's insistence on keeping us safe and small. May we learn to receive love from the universal heart of pure love itself, and give from that place.

May the arms of the Great Mother
Gather you into her soft holding.
May she who knows the struggle of the clay in you,
Breathe warm breaths on your tired eyelids.
May the low cradling of her right hand,
With feathered touch wipe your tears.
And may her gentle smile open the too-shut parts of you
Into Joy, and other forgotten melodies
Of sheer delight.
Seá

Glossary

I use the pronouns he/she and him/her interchangeably rather than the generic he/him throughout the book.

By teachings I refer to the Irish Celtic ways and customs.

archetype
That which presents itself to us as a living concept to magnify dispositions already in the psyche.

Brigit
The Celtic goddess.

Brigid
The saint.

consciousness
That which is awareness itself forever expressing, transforming, and expanding itself in and out of matter.

Earth-mind
That mind in us that has been conditioned through incarnating on the earth plane through culture, beliefs etc.

goddess/god
Genders given to facilitate the birthing of female/male archetypes within the human psyche.

magick
The spelling is the old feminine form.

Seá
As in Amen, Ho, So be it.

soul (anima)
Messenger of spirit; that which experiences our contracts on Earth. The life force that animates creation.

spirit (animus)
The original divine natural activator (DNA). Breath of all life.

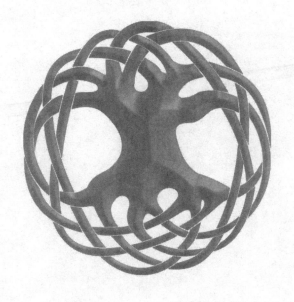

Introduction

Who am I?

WHO AM I
That fleshes your dreams to life?
That takes the breath from you
In your gallop to me?
Who am I that stirs
The tides in you
To fountains of spilling
Rainbows
And fills your starving eyes
With the bread of my mercy?
Ah! Child of fear-filled longing
Let me colour your tears
To match the red skies of your desires
And let the wrapping of my cloak
Of death sing you to life
So that the wild horse in you
Be tamed in the fierceness
Of my love...
— Brigit of the Celts

~

Anyone who has ever felt a yearning for something and not known how to name it,

Anyone who has ever felt the heart in them split open, and gallop beside them in fear or in ecstasy,

Anyone who has ever tasted the salt of their own deep grief
smarting their bones,
Anyone who has ever parched for that kind stream of mercy
to satisfy their thirsting,

Anyone who has ever called on death herself to gather them
in safe at last will not have to scrutinize these words in order
to understand them.
They will have lived them.

~

It is the soul in you bursting open, spilling your daily small cup of bless-ing into a chalice of overflowing beatitudes, offering to exchange your bread and water for a banquet spread for a queen. And it does not give up, it seduces through beauty and tenderness, through pain and distress, through sheer delight, and the deepest grief. It opens wide the parts that till now had no name, no real identity, that were withering away because of shame and guilt, the disowned parts. Eventually the poor confused earth-mind weakens, and once it does, it can only surrender. It has no case to offer. It can only come trembling on hands and feet, exhausted from the long, long winter of discontent, and surrender to the beloved, where the two become one, where even death cannot part them.

At this crucial time in the evolution of humankind it would appear that we are hungering for tender and functioning spirituality. Through the centuries we have been subjected to the harsh and commanding rules of an institutionalized so-called 'Mother Church', whose main objective was to control and condemn her children 'in the name of the Father'. Naturally this philosophy infiltrated social and cultural norms also, and 'for our own good' both church and state denied us that healthy self-knowing and self-trusting, the outcome of good role modelling.

We need to embrace both the soul, which has the properties of the feminine, and spirit, which manifests the properties of the masculine, because we need both. Our tendency is towards spirit (masculine): rea-son, understanding intellect, and goal setting; but we need to get to know our soul too. We create dichotomous thinking by dividing 'spiritual' into prayer, meditation, insight, and silence, and 'soulful' into the more expressive, such as feeling, creative, intuitive, spontaneous, sensual awareness. There is no such dichotomy. The dichotomy lies in the religious conditioning of the fathers of the church.

I believe that the soul in human beings has been uprising since the sixties especially. She is resurrecting; she is beginning to sing her own song of glory, using a language that touches the flesh of our hearts, and we can no longer hold out. The older ones amongst us are confused at our own inability to keep trusting the old credos. Somehow, many of us cannot match the answers in the catechism with the experience of our own blood, sweat, and tears. We need a more understanding and compassionate guidance that will listen to our cries, and our joys, and not abandon our wilderness experiences. I truly believe that the second coming of love flows through a more nurturing and flexible energy. It feels as if the 'old wooden cross', and insistence on subjugation of the body, is making way for the 'fountains of living waters' flowing in us. Form has to be willing to allow its clay body to soften so that a heart of flesh can breathe it alive. The old mindset is undergoing radical transformation, so that it can dance with paradox, feel at home with uncertainty, and with true alchemy, birth flowers from chaos.

I am not suggesting going back to the matriarchy, it is not going back at all, but a positive inclusion of the feminine, or soul, or anima energy as opposed to the insistence on a male God with male ideology and male power for a male populace. Brigit, that pre-Christian Celtic goddess, typifies soul energy today in the hearts of men and women. For this great blessing I give thanks. In this book, it appears that I concentrate on this energy, but that is of no consequence at all, for the power of soul consciousness transcends personalities, gender, and ages. Soul can easily be named Hildegard, Magdalene, Jesus, or even Bob Geldof. She can also be named in the smile of your child, in the love making with your partner, in the tears of your grief, in the howls of your despair. She is named by whatever brings expression to life: 'All naming of me limits my gifts, call me by the skin that fleshes your own Soul.'

It is time to grow up spiritually, and no longer look to a divine inbodiment out there for our salvation or approval. Time has come for us to name ourselves holy, with the encouragement of the divine feminine represented by our own souls which claims no hierarchy.

For a while we will consider the Brigit archetype of soul, and the understanding of the relationship between soul and our earth-mind. We may then more fully comprehend this part of us that had to trade the earth language of experience for the cerebral theory of Logos. We had to exchange the poetry of lover for the sterile script of dogma, and something green in us withered, something brilliant in us dimmed, something living in us died. We needed to be called forth, to be delightfully seduced; and we were shamed instead. We asked for bread, and we got stones. Now, the face of the feminine has returned to soften the hard rains that poured their acid on our inner pastures. We had to split from our own inner wisdom to accept beliefs alien to our intuition, alien to our own definition of holy, and we became weary fighting a part of ourselves, known as ego/earth-mind, that somehow we knew never meant to harm us. It simply reiterated the messages it received from the condemning voice of a merciless conditioning.

Shantideva (Buddhist master) maintained that the mind is a battlefield in which we have to use the sword of discrimination to kill off all negativity. This battlefield language does not heal. If we live by the sword, that is, if we use violence in any form it kills off the vital source of love itself.

Soul in all her splendour, soul in all her wilderness, soul in all her terracotta richness is coming home in us and through us. The days of confrontation, control, earth raping, discrimination, war mongering, warring language will all wear themselves out. The medals of old outdated victories will rust in their shabby and dusty boxes, the triumphant battle cries will not be so loud, and the justification for revenge and retaliation will no longer be excused. Fear will have its last raging tantrum, and will then fall exhausted into the arms of love, as we human beings become more conscious. We are all responsible for that day.

All the holy practices, of all the holy people, count as naught if they have not helped in the transformation of fear into love. All the foreign teachings, translated for our edification cannot reach the heart of man if they are interpreted into a language that serves our intellects alone.

The tottering legs of the old men of 'hell-fire' and 'damnation' and academic spirituality will break, will tumble and fall, as the earth herself will no longer carry them. The fish of Pisces have to turn towards the water carrier, Aquarius, and follow the waxing and waning of the moon, if they are to enjoy the full flow of the tides. It is as if the old laws can no longer stand. Moses has to exchange his commandments of stone for the comforting cloak of beatitude. Magdalene stands on the altar, dressed in her purple stole of sacred office, golden and red flowing dress magnifying her woman's passionate breasts. She offers sacrifice, not a human one to a God of wrath, but to the earth, in the rich sweet spices, exotic fruits, and aromatic oils – the harvest of our own homecoming. An ode to love will be heard above the self-hypnotic rhyming of the 'seven deadly sins' or long worn-out confessions of '*mea culpa, mea culpa, mea maxima culpa*'.

The faithful are no longer content with a theology that insists on hierarchy, and are becoming less faithful to the 'faith of our fathers'. They are tuning into the voice of the universal mercy that embraces all. The roaring lions in the pulpit now have to lie with the lambs they led to slaughter and learn from them a new gospel, a gospel of humility to include self-honouring, respect for nature, and joy.

Attributes of Brigit

Goddess Brigit (synonymous with soul) was known amongst the Celts as the 'mother of all greening things', and was the protector of the animal, plant, and human kingdoms. Ritual was her forte, and it is in ritual that the language of symbols and soul unite to form a mighty catalyst of healing. She is bringing sacred ceremony and ritual back into our daily living to show us the richness and the blessedness in all aspects of our precious lives. There is a rite of passage for every transition in life; and ritual that is witnessed, is twice blessed. Creation hails and appraises the transformatory element within the expression of sacred rites.

Brigit was said to understand the symbolic language of animals, newborn children, and the dying. Her poetry seemingly came from the 'places where the rivers in Ireland find their source'. Her words were as a sweet balm to those in need of comforting, and likewise were a source of challenge and persuasion to those who appeared lazy in their soul's harvesting. (Later, St. Brigid was imbued with these same attributes.)

Though the Celtic peoples worshipped the pre-Christian goddess, Brigit, my belief is that her time of greatness is now. She is able to both speak out loudly and whisper her teachings and wisdom to those who are willing and sensitive enough to hear them above the monotonous dirge of cerebral outpourings. Her strong love, tough at times, encourages humans to be steadfast in the face of persecution, political unrest, and fear stemming from media propaganda. It was said that her mantle of peace and love spreads itself across the universe and gathers all into its gentle impartial cradling.

Creation cycles

Nothing is documented regarding Celtic belief systems. This is because the Celts did not believe in writing down anything. All teachings were oral. Despite this, I have tried to reach an intuitive understanding of things by remembering the mythology, *scealta* or 'stories' handed down to us. Most of these stories I have learned through the medium of Irish or Gaelic, and no doubt the Irish love to tell the story, and add their bit too. 'A good story is like the rosary', my Nanny would say, 'it has the trimmings', meaning it needs to have a bit added to it every time.

It is however clear that the Celts believed that life itself had a certain rhythm or cycle. One full cycle of breath took millions of years so that the Great Spirit breath is still creating its evolutionary creation on the earth, and in all worlds creation is ongoing. Nothing is static; all is in constant transformation like the circulatory system of the heart. (See *The Unfinished Universe*[i].)

The following is the story of creation I have been taught as has actually been experienced psychically through such poetic eyes, the eyes of my ancestors.

Creation myth:
the beginning of the spiral

We do not live on earth; we live in earth. Deep in the clay of earth we take our form. Spirit is in form in us. Back into clay we become again, and again, and again. Clay is our skin, our home, and the sacred breath enlivens our clay to life. The Great Spirit breathed in and inspired all life. The out breath is the moulding of the clay to form. To experience life in all its forms is the work of each individual soul that comes from breath. Here is a story of creation that supports our soul journeys.

This creation myth should be told aloud sitting beside a big open fire with friends gathered and only the candle light to light the evening darkness.

Great Spirit or Great Birther of all fell into love with the spacious sky that streamed from its breath and the blue watery bed below that gathered from its tears of joy. After millions and millions of ages beholding its wonders, it smiled a smile so bright that a golden ball of fire glowed from the right eye, and another ball of shining silver from the left eye, and together they lit up the wide spaces above the waters, and saw their reflection smile from them.

Millions and millions of stars and galaxies flung themselves across the blue sky; such was their delight. The great eye took them all into its sight as its heart broke and split wide open when it beheld the beautiful colours of the waters below and the strong majesty of the great stones that rose out of their mouths. Time and much time passed, and all it could do was open wider and wider the beating heart to such beauty. It was grateful to the great eyes for sharing such marvelous sights.

As it fell deeper into love with all that appeared, suddenly movement trembled in the waters and green life shot up from the undergrowth. Flowing tears of joy reached the dry lands and more and more vegetation and flora appeared on the surface of the earth, until soon all was adorned like a wondrous magick carpet of startling colours. Its big heart swelled as it beheld the red-brown earth below and the open spaciousness of the sky above. Soon the mist from its eyes drew rainbows across the wide expanse of sky and music most delightful filled the ether. It beheld the wondrous dance of all and as the gasses erupted from the great stones that sat in the waters, multitudes of flaming red and orange particles threw themselves at the sky, and fell to the earth with a sound that echoed all over the waters below and above.

As these gigantic pieces of stone fell in the earth space, they themselves created much sound and movement. When this dance was over the great heart opened even further, as it beheld the experiencer of all inspiration for it was called *Beatha* or 'Life' or 'Soul'. It was Soul who would inspire the creation of even more and more beauty and delighted to be the experiencer of all inspiration.

When Spirit beheld Soul's exquisite smile, joy overflowed so much that flowers and herbs adorned the red earth, and life and movement shuddered in the waters below. Spirit reached towards Soul with great and utter honouring of such delicate energy yet strong heartbeat. From the deepest respect within it spoke these words:

'From the breath in me I call you to me. You, the beloved of my heart, the out-breath of my being; I bow to your majesty and with all the love of creation I behold your beauty. Will you, rhythm of my own breath, unite with me and be the beat of my own heart in all the worlds of our creation? With great rejoicing in your steadfastness and love I name you *Anam uilíoch* (Oversoul).'

With the happiness of a bride on her wedding day, Soul, out-breath of Spirit in-breath, experiencer of all his inspiration, *Anam*, drew close to Great Spirit breath; together they smiled on all natural things and continued to manifest their wonders and delights. Time and time passed until, eventually, human beings were birthed. Their next of kin, animal, stood by them, and consciously agreed to be the lesser amongst them, and serve humans in whatever way they could. Human beings gave great thanks to the animal kingdoms and together they breathed in harmony until they became upset because the humans perceived the animals were not serving sufficiently. From then on there was friction amongst them and soon fighting and ravaging broke out. Then fear grasped the heart of man because he realized that the animal had more body strength than he, and this made him very defensive. Since then the two kingdoms have not engaged so much together.

All the time Oversoul spoke to the heart of man but he refused to listen. It agreed that it would simply whisper in his heart now and again and show him a happier way to be with all of nature. Overoul also agreed to send a personal Soul or *Anam* guide to each created form that was named, so that they could live and move and have their beingness within its care. Once a breath of the Great Spirit came to earth as human, they could come as many times as they needed in order to learn to live in harmony with all creation and their personal Soul would agree to come with them every time.

This was a wondrous gift, as no one had to feel alone. Oversoul longed for humans to live fully and enjoy the abundance of such a rich world. The work of personal Soul or *Anam* guides was to help mankind to experience their lives, in tune with all without fear. Spirit loves to manifest in the earth as this is an outpouring of love. And this is our task to be the outpourers of divine love.

From chaos to creativity

We have many transformations to go through. What we call chaos and disarray can be translated as movement, change, and transformation at work. All is important. Nothing is accident. All is towards homeostasis. All is perfect.

No doubt all history of Celtic cosmology is mythic; and the one I just told is just as believable as the accepted biblical creation story. A myth touches the soul and enlivens an ancient cellular memory, which cannot be understood by reason only because it is sensory, rather than intellectual. The koan used by meditationists to transcend the ordinary min. The poet Amergin, also known as Merlin the Druid, wrote a poem about the oneness of all creation, which included the hypnotic, the translogical rhythm of paradox. Hannah also has a poem reiterating the same:

> *Who is she that breathes fire into my bones,*
> *and throws the stars across the sky?*
> *Who is she that greens the boughs and frangrances the flowers?*

Who is she that warms my days and lights my nights?
Who is she that flows seductively in streams
and pounds relentlessly in rivers?
Who is she that chisels the stones
and throws up mountains to climb?
I am she who breathes fire in my bones
and travels the galaxies
I am she who greens my life
and she who trails my fragrance
I am she who cradles my dark and light;
the seductress of all
I am the stones, the earth and the mountains
I am she...
— *Hannah Cunningham*

This inclusion of oneself with the whole of creation is the heart of the Celts. This was a living, breathing relationship whereas Buddhism, whilst embracing all of creation did not make all of nature its primary teacher.

The middle way was the way of the Celts, and Buddha taught likewise with the emphasis on moderation. This middle way or way of non-extremism showed itself in the way in which the universe was depicted by our ancestors. The universe was perceived as being divided into layers, these being:

Sky world – of constellations, moon, sun, stars, galaxies. Place of high gods and goddesses – place of magick making, spirit world, the wind, rain, snows, sky creature's creator of healing, breath of the story

Earth world – animals, plants, human beings, mountains, healing herbs, place of footprints, birthplace of spirit, formed phenomena, rivers, seas, movement

Underworld – ancestors, healing, bones, darkness, non-action, stillness, death, origins of life, mystery

The earth world, the place where we ground the divine is the middle place, the place between the upper and lower worlds. This does not mean that humans cannot visit these places if they so will. Meditation, visualization, yoga, pain, day dreaming, dissociation all take us from the middle place to either of the other worlds. The non-psychotic is able to 'come home again', back into present time. The neurotic often stays there and has to be helped to return. People known as soul retrievers are able to help others back into the middle place, having retrieved parts of themselves from other worlds.

Violence and religion

Do we still need crucifixes with or without images of violence? Do we still need to contemplate the victimization of a man over and over, and in so doing heap yet more blame and guilt on an overly contrite people? Do we still need a brutal onslaught on our already over-taxed consciousness? Does the patriarchy still need to emphasize victimization and misdirected emotionalism? The images of Jesus dying a torturous death on a crude cross do not help free the soul from darkness. I suggest to the contrary, that such grotesque images including the so-called stations of the cross in Catholicism, (contemplating the journey from Gethsemane to Golgotha), and the bleeding, innocent lamb of God carrying the shadow projections of the so-called 'faithful' do not open the hearts of people. On the contrary they lead to morbidity, depression, and self-abuse. This often manifests in self-wounding as displayed in the practices of contemplative religious orders.

This emphasis on victimization and cruelty in religion might suggest latent sexual dysfunctioning. The overpowering father stereotype is an age-old image of the dysfunctioning family system. Desertion of the father is typical patriarchal abandonment psychology.

Inappropriate paternal control arises from a need for total authority. To appease the father's anger, the son is sacrificed according to the utilitarian dogma of 'for the good of others'. We continue to sacrifice our sons by sending them to war, for the good of the whole. They become saviours of our world; and 17 year olds are sacrificed in places like Iraq and Afghanistan, all in the name of patriarchal politics.

Holy consciousness no longer prescribes to the continuing of such abusive religious fanaticism and abusive beliefs. If God so loved the world that he sent his only begotten son to die for the sins of humanity, so that He could be appeased, then we refuse to bow to, and recognize such a tyrant. Mothers like Mary nowadays are silenced into their grief and help-lessness, as their sons are led like lambs to the slaughter, to die to save their country. The Calvary story has been the lynch pin to which the Church of Rome has attached great importance. The natural outcome within the psyche of humanity is self-disgust, guilt, and helplessness. Soul wounding coming from such beliefs becomes too heavy a load to carry and many dump their shadow and sinful selves on the shoulders of others. Thus wars are created on the battlefield of projected fear. Fear of the enemy without creates fearsome and fearful entities in our world. As long as the church talks of demons roaming the world seeking whom they may destroy, we will have terrorism, terrorized people projecting fear.

Perhaps it is time to let dogma die. One cannot replace one theological principle with another – they are all philosophical principles. The true meaning of philosophy comes from the Greek, *philo* and *sophos*, meaning 'love' and 'wisdom'. Wisdom does not grow with principles or dogmas. It grows with compassion, applied healing experiences, choice, order, indi-viduation, and love. Time for commandment is past. Time of hierarchy of holiness is past. Time now is for the everyday person to earth the divine in their bodies, in their personal experience of the holy one. Time to grow up and leave the house of commandment; to lift each other up out of the hell of so-called sinfulness. Time to live the dance of bounty.

It is our individual task, our purpose on the earth to ground the divine in our own being. It is no longer the prerogative of a church to dictate how, where, and when. For some it will be in the place of work, and for others in the way they teach, whilst for others in the way they rear their children. Indeed, the fact that you are a living being means you ground the divine in all you think, say, and do. It is not for an elitist club. It is time to come out of the University of the Intellect alone, and open the heart to love, and mutual respect in the market place. University is for the elite, the intellectual, for writing of thesis, reading books and accumulat-ing degrees. This is the old way of acquiring knowledge. It is time to walk our spiritual talk, to walk wisdom, not preach it. It's time to stop writing and learning about spirituality, and start living with soul. It is time to stop believing in Buddha, in Christ, in gurus, but to be Buddha, be the Christ, here and now today for ourselves, in our own family, in our community, in the bus queue, and in the wider reaches of the world.

The first truth of Buddhism is that all life is *dukka* (suffering). According to Celtic Consciousness all life is a gift, a celebration, a mystery, a wonder. Buddha also saw that clinging to life becomes suffering. When we can fully experience life, and let it go, we can find joy, as joy is the flip side of suffering. In the face of human ageing, illness, and death Buddha was fired into finding a way out of this terrible predicament. In search of a philosophy, a path to 'happiness', which might ensure this outcome, he left home, leaving his newborn son and wife in the middle of the night, we are told. Many women have had to experience the irresponsibility of the male who goes off to search for his *nirvanha*, as the responsibility of family lies too heavily on their shoulders. Buddha left home to find liberation for all. Jesus left home to find salvation for all. It seems as though liberation could not be found within the family setting. Buddha himself maintained that women would have brought blight to his order. Catholicism still refuses women ordination. Naturally, Buddha and Jesus had a more altruistic reason for leaving their families, and 2,500 years later we Westerners are still trying to grasp many of their teachings on suffering.

Jesus the Christ was discriminated against because of his relationship, sexual or otherwise, with Mary Magdalene. Buddha maintained that women could not find *nirvanha* because woman herself was an obstacle on the path to liberation. This is the oppressive abusive dogma that women have had to live with for too long.

Like Buddhism, the old Celtic wisdom believes in speaking out against oppression, against abuse in society, against political aggressors, against abuse of nature. However, we as Celts believe that there is a time for all things, therefore, a time for old age is natural, and as such is to be embraced. It is a time of deeper involvement with soul values; a decathexing from the outer, and a joyful concentration on the internal landscape; the integration of the whole of life.

Acceptance of the pain, staying with it, being with its limitations, while still expanding more and more into life is to live without suffering. Therefore, death is not fearfully anticipated, but is grown into through living life fully. It is the natural letting go of form so that the soul may be free. Buddha believed that escape from the continuous wheel of life and death, from the darkness of ego mind, could be attained in the destroying of the ego, thus going beyond illusion to live in the luminous light of *nirvanha*. The world of illusion had to be transcended so that pain and suffering could be eradicated. Happiness and light, therefore, would be the outcome.

Jesus the Christ encouraged us to daily take up and embrace our pains, and follow the way of love. From his agony on the cross Jesus taught that separation from self, from love itself was the deepest pain. He clearly showed us that when we accept the cross, pain, when we integrate the pain of life and death daily, there is full liberation from suffering. Fear is the element within pain that separates us from all that is love.

Celtic teachings do not talk of eradication of the dark 'ego/earth-mind', but the compassionate integration of both light and dark. Spirit, sky, light, out of body, mind transcendence, escaping our natural feelings cannot lead us to holiness (wholeness). Flesh, birth, death, womb, the dark, earth, the undergrowth, nature, winter, dark moon, blood, pain, the stuff of our earthedness which, when attended to, and given full recognition, leads to joy, love, congruence, at-one-ment, in oneself and all around, wherever our feet may tread, in the here and now. Woman in-bodies such wholeness. At birth, especially, women go through the pain barrier, feel it, and naturally transcend it after which trauma comes joy and ecstasy. Woman naturally goes beyond ordinary mind in birthing. Religion, with only spirit and light, is not a religion for women, or for men who have embraced the earth this time.

The time is now in this age for 'the second coming', time for East and West to merge to produce an integrated force, a messiah, not newborn and vulnerable, but a strong, mighty alliance. Before this transformation can happen, a time of transition has to take place. That time is now. We have been in labour, and now the waters are breaking, and we are poised and ready.

Buddhism without soul and Christianity without discipline of the mind are each like a bird with only one wing. They cannot soar alone. We need the marriage of both if we are to experience the earthing of the divine love in us. Celtic Consciousness talks about a need for the merging of animus and anima, earth-mind with soul, soul with spirit; the tri-une. In the mighty alliance of Buddha nature, which is compassion through discipline, and the Christ nature, which is compassion through love in action, we have both wings with which to soar. May this age of the merging of Buddha and Christ within ourselves transform our small earthen minds into the mind of the creator; the mind of the divine. Then our souls can soar. Then our hearts can burst open into the pure joy of being. We are all responsible for this time and it is now time to live mindfully so that we can die consciously. This alone will ensure the ever-lasting abundance of life, the real *nirvanha*; an end to all conceptual thinking.

The Jesus archetype

LIVE ONLY LOVE
He came to walk the earth.
He felt all that we feel.
He was vulnerable and strong.
He knew that he had come to heal and be healed.
And the message that he brought,
And the lessons that he taught,
Were full of healing words
That touched the hearts of those
In fear, so they could hear. When he said;
'Open wide your hearts to each experience.
Go beyond your fears,
Through the grief of endless years,
You're not alone,
For I have come,
To live only LOVE.
When you can love yourself
No judgement and no blame.
When you forgive your wrongs
Then you can treat each other just the same
In mercy's name.
And we say:
'We'll open wide our hearts, to each experience.
We'll go beyond our fears,

Through the grief of endless years,
We're not alone,
For we have come,
To live only LOVE.
— *P. Anam-Áire*[ii]

Jesus the man, the archetypical lover of all things, the very human being, is alive in the hearts of many and offers abundance, the 'bounty full dance' of life here and now; but if we do not add our experience with his, then we deny our own divinity. His soulfullness, his feminine Brigit self was never truly acknowledged by the fathers of the church. They preached a theology of dualism, the humanness of Jesus the victim as opposed to the omnipotence of Jesus the god. His deeply feeling self, his insecurities, his very human longings, his neediness of a functioning father role model, his love of woman, his love of man, his anger and frustration, his need to be loved, his fear of aloneness were seen as his humanness divorced from his god self. The god part, the fact he was the Son of God, his miracle making, his resurrection, his ability to heal and pray long hours, his raising people from the dead, and especially his seeming androgynous self. All of this separated him from us mere human beings. After all he was the mediator between God and us, as our humanness was sinful because of our so-called 'family of origin', namely Adam and Eve.

Jesus the god and Jesus the human being were isolated parts of ourselves which were never encouraged to integrate, and so a dualistic illusionary idol was our guide for life. Furthermore, as good Christians, the violent death Jesus endured, his grief in the garden of olives, and his great suffering were our responsibility. Unless we repented and owned our sinful self we could not be healed. Jesus was preached at us rather than introduced to us as a fellow traveler, who transmitted great universal truths through the medium of storytelling. The wise words he spoke were neither dogmatic nor theological, but depicted everyday life as lived by the everyday people with whom he lived and worked. Jesus brought back the language of feelings of symbology of soul: the wilderness feelings of raw aloneness and abandonment, of grief beyond what his frail humanity could bear, of love that allowed him to embrace women.

Soul language got lost in the theology of law keeping and commandments. He was the gospel, the good story; the story of human predicament and human courage. His was the language of the lover, but the fathers of the church had to translate his simple words into an intellectual thesis, which they then could interpret to control an ignorant, erring populace.

Jesus walks hand in hand with the goddess archetype. Now his message of love is heard above the rusting rules of the 'old men of the cloth'. His stories are being told not with the accompanied fanfare of pomp and glory but through the everyday courageous lives and longings, failures and heartbreaks, joys and delights of real feeling human beings irrespective of religious affiliation.

Embodiment of teachings

Jesus embodied Buddha's teachings. They both now hold the chalice to your mouth and invite you to drink from the cup of your own precious life. They both smile on you, child of grace, and welcome you to your soul-self. You have been too long in the confessional prison. Buddha says: 'Live your life for others; learn the teaching that all is illusion and that the ego mind is the greatest illusion of all'.

Jesus looks on you and says: 'I have taken on a body for the soul (sole) purpose of showing you how to live abundantly in yours'. Brigit invites you to fully experience your days so that you may die in joy of having lived them all. Wisdom embraces the feminine face of love and finds expression in you and your children's children to the fourth generation.

Buddha holds the archetype of functioning animus, the holy trinity of Youth, Father, and Wise Man. Jesus holds that of anima, Virgin, Mother, and Crone. Brigit who is anima also expresses the attributes of Youth, Father, and Wise Man. Each age must embody the teachings of the previous age in order to expand them so that transformation may emerge. May we bring the wisdom of ages and birth it into a 'new' form with courage and love.

Sacred marriage

With the strongest love our Celtic ancestors call us by our own name. They call us to ourselves and they not only honour our human predicament but call it holy. They say:

You are the holy hearth of the Beloved,
That place where the Beloved sits,
With his feet in the warm ashes of your welcoming,
Eats the corn bread from your hands
And with his right ear near your face, listens to your stories.
— P. Anam-Áire

They see our humanness as: 'The rich brown clay of your own holiness, the building site for the house of love.' All grace is to be found in this human clay. They advise: 'Claim your human self for it is a place higher than the unbodied beings (angels).' In other words, look neither up nor down, only look inwards to your soul, and from there look out. For too long we have been trying to transcend the body, to kill off our bad and sinful earth-mind. Now it is time to claim it and take responsibility for our own enlightenment, not in spite of, but through and because of our incarnation.

What is enlightenment but soul seducing earth-mind to unite with her, to come down, down into the clay place of the heart of love with her, and be warmed in the fire of love's total acceptance. In this open place of non-judgement, we begin to see our frightened selves through the eyes of love:

EYES OF LOVE
Through the eyes of love all is perfect,
Through the eyes of love we are free,
Through the eyes of love we are innocent,
I am you and you are me.
(The soul and ego mind unite)
— P. Anam-Áire[iii]

Naturally the poor ignorant earth-mind will fight this interfering pursuer with all its might. For it knows that when it eventually gives way, the personality will never be the same again. And this is the grief, the letting go of the way things used to be, the safe guarded predictable 'yellow brick road' of goal setting and end gaining. In fear and trembling the impoverished ego cries to the personality that it has helped to form and maintain:

> *Have I not kept you safe in the past?*
> *See how my guardianship of you*
> *Has created good strong defenses against pain.*
> *Why risk this security?*
> *Why trade this known home*
> *For a gypsy caravan of unpredictability?*

In the past the patriarchy preached at us about the evilness of the earth-mind and how we had to subdue it, fight it, and make it subject to spirit. The fathers of the church, together with philosophers of that age, warned us to be in fear and dread of it. The Brigit archetype, however, encourages us to see it as an impoverished, well-intentioned dear old-fashioned relative, who needs to come in from the cold and be warmed at our hearts.

The message of Brigit is not written on stone nor is it written at all, save in the innate knowing of truth in the deepest recesses of the universal soul of humanity.

Chapter 1

Love

Love according to the teachings

BELOVED
The lilt of the music
Danced across the air
Like a free floating seed
On the thermals of life
And my soul stirred
Passionately embracing the lover
In the warmth of its breath
You and I, at one
In love, and the lover
— *Hannah Cunningham*
January 2006

According to the teachings, our natural state is love, which is Divine or Spirit. If our natural state is spiritual, then it is erroneous to say that I am becoming more spiritual. Our task is to let go of our limitations, our fears, our insecurities, and self-doubt, so that the flow of divine spirit can pour from our beingness, and pure love can infiltrate us, unhindered and uninhibited.

Love is about… order and chaos, reason and paradox, structure and spontaneity, continuity and change. Love incorporates everything and all. It is about disorder as it is about order. It includes all the many colours of the spectrum of life. Everything will return to divine love in the end, and that love is the unconditional regard of the divine for humanity. Nothing is outside this love. Our earthed love has to have all its expressions in human beings in order to reach wholeness. Eventually, this love will be integrated into divine love so that only pure love or unconditional love will be expressed. We have to find love through separation, truth through untruths, power through our vulnerability, our divinity through our humanness, compassion through our anger, joy through our fear, and holiness through our brokenness.

Often what we call love is nothing more than sentimentality or possession. When love is not accompanied by transformation it is not love, but dependency. We depend on love remaining static. In our finite minds it alone is not allowed to falter. It has to be as it was this time last year. The thought of it changing immediately produces feelings of fear and dread. It is a drug that keeps us from feeling depressed, from looking at the darkness of our shadows. If someone loves me, I must be OK. This love has to carry people in times of difficulty and pain. 'If I did not have you, I would be dead; your love for me keeps me alive.' This type of dependency, this parent/child relationship and addiction is also erroneously called real love in society. I have realized through my own addiction i.e. to being right – arrogance that addiction means mist guided self-love; in other words, looking in inappropriate places for satisfaction.

Love as seen from the Cauldron is what keeps everything, and all, in motion and transformation in the universe.

Love it is that transforms the pupae into the wings of the butterfly.
Love it is that shrinks the soul small enough to fit into the
confines of matter.
Love it is that calls the soul from the encasement of the body to a
wider view of itself.
Love it is that gives the sparkling colours to the rainbow.
Love it is that helps the snowdrop push itself up, up through
the hard ground of winter to where it can see the sun.

Love it is that imbues all life with passion and might.
Love it is that thunders in the stormy sky and throws sparks
to the waters.
Love it is that fuses the molecules and atoms, and produces
organisms to live and multiply, and grow, and change.
Love it is that destroys the mountains with volcanoes and eruptions.

Love it is that takes the life force from the baby before it has formed in the womb.

Love it is that creates friction and electricity, and fires that burn the earth's face.
Love it is that turns all things in the universe upside down so that you can forget your everyday mind, and move, and dance in a spiral of creativity.
Love longs for you to accept your wilderness and crazy making as much as you accept your structured thinking.
Love it is that takes your well thought-out plans and foundations, and crashes them all in one teardrop.
Love it is that shows you the foolishness of your ways, and asks you to be with them as you are with your serious certainties.

Love it is that allows you to see the so-called mistakes of another, and asks you to throw them to the sky.
Love it is that lets you touch the mystery of another human being, and allows you to move closer to their humanness.
Love it is that opens your eyes to the insufficiency of another so that your soul can bypass them, and you can say yes, yes, yes to life, and to one another.
Love it is that whispers your name in your ear when you have forgotten who you are.
Love it is that tears your heart asunder in the reshaping of it.

Love it is that speaks goodbye for you when your voice can hardly take in the grief of parting.
Love it is that reminds and rehearts you to the smile of the beloved when she is no longer with you.
Love it is that stands in your heart, and shouts out loud 'I am beautiful', even when you do not feel it.
Love it is that destroys all hopes in you, so you can be hopeless and surrender to joy. And love is not an easy lover.
She demands all and everything from you the beloved. She asks you to be ready for greatness but you have to get rid of your l iming views first.

Love will take you to the edge of your small self, and hurl you at the stars.

Are you willing to be transformed by pure love so that your earth love may be absorbed by its inspiration? The choice is yours.

Love and boundaries

OVERFLOW
The wells of grief
Cannot contain the overflow of sorrow
And joy is but a speck
In the distant past
For where love cannot touch
No healing will begin
And life starves into death
— *Hannah Cunningham*
  January 2006

Modern psychologists would advocate that lovers create safe psychological boundaries, thus ensuring that the other never really knows the deeper levels of one's psyche. When we can know ourselves, when we allow divine love to flow in, and through us, we are free from the fear of being overpowered, and our boundaries are loosened. When you love, you open not only your heart but your being to the other. This total vulnerability allows lessons to be learned, love to be reciprocated, healing to happen, and souls to fuse and dance a new dance, no longer ever lonely again, but at peace with aloneness.

So what is it to love someone? Language is limiting. When we have a heart connection with another we have a wish or longing to be near them. It is a matter of 'I feel better when you are here, so please do not leave.' This love is very subjective and confined to the lover and beloved only. There is no room for the universal, just you and me, and 'make the world go away' syndrome. But is this loving someone else or simply loving this feeling it produces in you. Is it all so subjective?

Detached love

Detached love would seem to be a contradiction in terms. Can I really love deeply and still be detached? If I love in a detached way, does this mean that I am not involved with the other, or that I have stopped caring? To detach would seem to infer a moving away from, no longer part of, or bonded to. Is this not the antithesis of love itself? If I love in a detached way, can I still be with you in a committed way, and care for you, or does it mean that I no longer wish for this closeness with you, so I do not share deeply who I am. Surely, this is the opposite of love, this is fear of intimacy. Jesus the Christ said, we should love each other as we love ourselves. This seems a difficult task. Surely, I cannot love myself in a detached way or I would neglect my own life, but to detach does not mean to neglect. It does not mean not to care; it does not mean lack of intimacy. It means that I am free to love you without the neediness to either fix you to my standards, or control you. I loved my ex-husband in the beginning naturally. The marriage grew but I didn't. When he did not meet my standards I fell out of love. Clearly, my love was totally conditional. I love you if ...

To love in a detached way is to love and care just as deeply and passionately, but without trying to possess the beloved. You are not my property. You are free, and in this free space you choose to be with me, and love me. This is the wonder. To detach is to lay less emphasis on the personality, and concentrate on the soul values. It means that the beloved is free to be itself without having to change to meet my needs. Jesus and Buddha were able to be with so many people because their love was detached, impersonal. They were not involved with the personality but with the deeper journey of the self, or soul; the unchangeable, the divine nature. They were an *anam-aire*, a 'soul-carer', an *anam-cara*, a 'soul friend'. I have also found this easier – to love generally in a detached way. The difficulty comes for me in an intimate relationship with a special other. Personalities are difficult to live with. Seems we have to see through the mask right through to the divine indweller in each other. When two become one, as relationship is often defined, personality must surely be dissolved into the beloved, the divine within the two.

When we love in a detached way, ie not soley attached to the person-ality, we see the fruits of the spirit in the other, and we are less in love; rather, we become love, and are free to love universally; no confines, no limitations. I am not talking of 'free love' as freedom to choose different sexual partners, which of course is not love, but lust, and satisfies only the earth-mind's pleasure at the time.

> *BIRTH*
> *What births the heart*
> *Over and over*
> *Is its willingness*
> *To open into*
> *It's longing*
> *For love*
> *And be*
> *The love it seeks*
> — *P. Anam-Áire*

Woman has a deep yearning to bond with her lover. She is willing to merge so that her anima can find harmony with her opposite, animus. If however, her animus is immature, this yearning becomes dysfunctioning and possessive. She will then have a need to own the other, to absorb his maleness, in order to fill up what is 'wanting' in her psyche. When her own animus finds expression in her life, it protects, guides, and clarifies her visions. She no longer needs to obsess over her outer male, but can love him from a more detached place of pure love. She doesn't need him so she is free to experience love in, with, and through him.

Likewise, with man, when he awakens to his own female-ness, his own anima, or soul, and allows her creative power to colour his life, he no longer needs to own his lover. He no longer has a need for her to nur-ture and mother him, as he will be fed by the self-loving juices of his own anima. When two such individuals come together, male and female, they are free to love with clarity, and intimacy. They come from a place of wholeness within themselves.

The same may be said about homosexual people. It is important that they cultivate these energies and integrate them within themselves also; otherwise they seek for such completion in the other.

Fundamentally, love would seem to expresses itself in two ways:

— the obvious
— the symbolic

Obvious ways

The obvious ways are known to us as we have been conditioned to accept them thus. No one can easily accept that discomfort and brokenness can also be some of the guises love wears. The good heart feelings people share alone or in nature or together either in a family setting, friendships, or the love between lovers are some of the obvious manifestations of love. These are situations where our hearts widen and our souls rejoice, and expand in consciousness. We must remember that love visits us through the medium of symbols and mystery too, so we need to awaken to such phenomena or we will totally miss the more obscure, nonetheless valid messages of love on a day-to-day basis.

Symbolic ways

The language of divine love is the language of the unconscious, and the unconscious reveals itself mysteriously. We have to practise seeing with the inner eye of perception, and hear with the inner ear of the soul in order to awaken to love's still-small voice.

Our souls are forever guiding us towards expansion of consciousness to include the non-verbal, non-active, non-logical, and non-rational ways of knowing. The work of the soul in us is to bring us to the end of our earth-mind's assumptions, and calculations in order to draw us deeper and deeper into the well of our own mysteries. This work includes a deeper awareness of synchronicity, and so-called coincidences. The latter is usually defined as 'accidental occurrences'.

According to the soul there is another way of interpreting such coincidences. When we are visited by a health problem we immediately look for cures, or a quick way to relieve the pain. This is normal. Pain is seen as a kind of accident. It is viewed as a bother, and a disaster in our daily hectic and success-orientated lives. The pain relief, (also known as pain killers), numb not only the painful feelings, but also the mind from considering other reasons.

PAIN
You can't kill pain, you have to feel it.
Respect the message and the messenger.
Don't say I'm on my way to recovery.
I only need to know the way
To uncover the healer under this pain.
I don't trust you if you kill the source of my healing.
You say I'll last another year if I take your medicine.
Let me tell you doctor I will last forever.
My healing has nothing to do with your medicine.
— Hannah Cunningham 2006.

Consciousness and pain

Naturally, there is another side we must consider and that is the patient needs to have control themselves while they are in a conscious state as to the amount, and frequency of pain relief they receive. Whilst working with a dying patient who felt she had lost all control of her life when admitted to the hospice, she shared with me that it was not the actual pain she was afraid of but the way they made a big deal when she asked for more morphine. I could hear the anger, the frustration, and the lack of self-autonomy, which added to her pain.

My friend Hannah, who presently has cancer in most of her body, maintains:

'As good as the McMillan nurses are, I am left with the feeling that control of my illness and my pain is their domain, not mine. It feels like

I have to almost plead for adequate pain medication, and justify my need for it. What happened to the "pain is what the patient says it is" philosophy? The concern on the part of the professionals is that my breathing may be affected, or levels of consciousness impaired. What do they think will happen? Maybe I will lose a few weeks of life in my body. The dying are living in the present moment, and when they need pain relief they need it now. They don't even want to discuss tomorrow's pain, tomorrow's needs. If they want the window open, they want it open now. They have no time for niceties or tidiness. I can be in the depths of despair at 10.00 a.m., and be fully in the place of joy at 10.15. Both are truths, and both are about living consciously.

'Is this the only reality there is? I have a belief that eventually we will all be able to choose which state or dimension of consciousness we live in. The higher levels of consciousness are available to me now as my body is loosening grip of earth consciousness, and my soul is taking me into a wider dimension than that of my body, which feels cramped, and suffocated. This is why I am opening windows at the moment, getting rid of furniture (to my husband's dismay), clearing spaces, and I know at a deep level it is my soul expanding its awareness.'

According to Freud we are only one tenth conscious. The more conscious we become the more questions we will ask from the pain. It is then not seen as a robber of our energy, but a messenger of grace asking us to take heed, to listen, to be aware of the internal environment that perhaps needs altering, or adjusting in some way.

As Hannah said, 'Pain is the calligraphy in my life, the beautiful script that demands my attention, even in the depths of misery with pain. The beauty of the internal script does not change because I feel pained.'

Maybe we have been ignoring our soul's need for joy, fun, and heartfelt love. Maybe we have been too attached to someone, and their departure fills us with dread and suffering. Maybe we continue to hold a grudge against someone ...whatever. If there is disquiet or disease within the mind, the body will manifest this. But remember the disease first started in the conditioned earth-mind, and the soul uses every situation possible to help us to change. She does not produce the pain but utilizes it to teach us about consciousness. Remember, the soul will not try and change you from something you really are intent on doing, even if this is to destroy your joy and hopes. *Your own free will decides.*

If you are conscious you will accept that everything you meet along the way is the Buddha or Christ energy. This is another way of saying that everything that shows up in your world is some kind of guide of love and compassion. Could this be said of pain? Think about it for a moment. If you judge the message, pain, and discriminate between a good message and a bad one, then you are not getting the point of soul. Your soul does *not* discriminate between good and bad. *Our soul uses everything to awaken us.*

It is so wonderful when we are visited by so-called 'good' messengers like getting a job with lots of money. Sometimes what happens is that we give our all to the job; we sell our souls for the thirty pieces of silver. So then our joy disappears, and we are breathing solely in order to get a promotion. As a result we never see our friends, never have a break to feed our souls, and our health deteriorates. We begin to get headaches or colon problems, or dermatitis, or the likes, and we wonder why our bodies should 'cheat' on us just when we need our strength for the work. Frustration sets in and we get depressed as we have to take days off work, and someone else is proposed for that promotion we had hoped for.

How can pain be a catalyst for healing? How can this situation possibly be a messenger of love?

As we become more conscious we will have no difficulty in seeing this, but if we are still seeing the situation as a personal catastrophe, which has little and nothing to do with love, then we need to take heed.

Love is the catalyst, the alchemist, the alchemy, and the very gold into which we can be transformed. But this transformation does not happen overnight, nor does it always feel like all sweetness and light. If love, the alchemist, has to transform our base metal, our earth-minds, into the golden mind of the Christ/Buddha/love, then we will have to go through a transformation, a change, a death, before the resurrection of our earth-minds. We are not too happy with any of these options as we associate transformation and death, with pain and suffering. What if we changed our associations regarding language? Supposing when we speak of death we consider using the word 'change/transformation' instead. When we speak of pain, we could substitute it with the word sensation without having to qualify it. When we have a bad day we could say we had an interesting day. Go on, try it and see what happens. The day is neutral;

life is neutral. *We* fill our days, *we* live our lives, the *day* is never bad, *life* is never bad; the way we choose to express it, colours our definition.

If language has its origin in thought patterns, i.e. the thought precedes the symbol (word), so the words we use symbolize thoughts, concepts, and ideas. It seems logical therefore that by changing our habitual thinking modes we can change the resultant language, and subsequent feeling modes. The reverse may just as well occur, i.e. by changing or modifying language we might just have different feelings, resulting in changed thought associations. Supposing the next time you are ill, can you imagine the following: instead of complaining that you have to stay in bed say to yourself 'It seems that I need a few days to be quiet. My body needs love and attention.'

Our souls invite us to experience our worlds, they have no attachments to outcomes, but the choices we make have consequences, and these produce love or fear. When we choose love we choose soulful living. But remember, if I invite love into my life she will challenge me to open to all that is not love, my fears, in the form of my insecurities, mistrusts, self-abandonment, hopelessness, failed dreams and losses. So be careful what you open into, and should you not open up your life you will be half alive, and afraid to die. If we are not in touch with our deeper mystery, we will miss out on the mysteries of love in nature, in physics, in the constellations, love in every form. In physics, love is the hidden miraculous energy, the unseen magickian who activates all seen and unseen phenomena. Love it is that fuses atoms and molecules, the very attraction between them, and love is the active merging element.

Anima –
functioning and dysfunctioning

Because the word 'animation' suggests vitality and movement, life itself is synonymous with soul, and is feminine. In order to live soulfully, lovingly on the earth we need to look at and understand the opposite, dysfunctioning anima.

Functioning anima (unconditioned)	Dysfunctioning anima (conditioned)
Loving – gives care	Caretakes, rescues, possessive
Creative – poetic, dancer etc.	Dreamer, Unearthed.
Takes risks – not afraid of change	Lives on the edge
Chaotic – can live with paradox	Unreliable
Natural – unsocialized	Rebels, dramatic
Willing to be in the dark – not knowing	Becomes morbid, helpless.
Is intuitive – listens to inner wisdom	No discernment
Listens to own rhythms – follows inner path	Self-absorption, selfish
Free child – loves to experience new things	Irresponsible, escapes life.
Simple – delights in life	Childish, refusing to grow up
Sensual gives mixed messages	Leaking sexuality,
Joyful	Inappropriate boundaries
Soul full – in touch with soul energy	No container.
Expressive	Over-indulgent – acts out

Animus –
functioning and dysfunctioning

Likewise, spirit or animus, considered masculine, has its dysfunctioning qualities.

Functioning animus *(unconditioned)*	**Dysfunctioning animus** *(conditioned)*
Loving – gives care	Caretakes, rescues, possessive
Container	Manipulates, controls
Present, stable	Immovable, intrusive
Activates	Drives, competes too much
Inner authority	Overpowering
Holy intelligence	Rationalizes too much
Discriminates	Judges, criticizes
Sets boundaries	Too rigid
Sexual	Obsessive, overpowering, impotent
Provides	Insists on caretaking
Guards	Possesses
Leads	Dictates, commands
Happy doing	Addicted to work
Spiritual	Dogmatic
Masculine	Butch/macho
Philosopher	Melancholic, conceptual
Disciplines	Strict, critical
Loves	Perpetrates

Chapter 2

Celtic Cauldron

Goddess versus saint

Goddess Brigit, worshipped by people of a sacred earth-imbued religion, was also known as Dana, who manifested the Virgin, Mother, Crone trinity (expressions of these important archetypes will be looked at later). Her father was Dagda, who was the guardian of the Cauldron of plenty, called the 'Undry'. He was the wise and honoured god of the *tuatha de Dannan* (the tribe of Dana). Because of her soul-filled grounded spirituality, Brigit is often associated with the spiritually and sexually explicit *Sheela-na-gig*, a Celtic goddess of fertility, who displayed her open vagina depicting her female splendour and passionate creativity. She also possessed within her the male organs of procreation. When viewed from a place of holy union and integration it is easy to see how the male penis, scrotum, and testicles replicate the vaginal passage to the womb and ovaries, thus forming the sacred union of soul and spirit or Cauldron of life from which creation flows.

It is specifically her stirring of the Cauldron of plenty, also known as Bronwyn's Cauldron, given to her by her father that impresses me. This gift to his daughter represents her initiation into womanhood, sexuality, and choosing a partner. The father's Cauldron of plenty and his belief in abundance fed his daughter with confidence to stir her own chalice. From this she knew her nature was not controlled, but contained. This stirring or circling the Cauldron can be explained also in psychological terms as working through our 'unfinished business', moving into individuation, and eventually reaching the place of liberation. This place of liberation was mythologically called *tír na-n-óg*, which is Gaelic for 'heaven' or 'place of eternal youth'.

In Hinduism we read of the churning of the ocean of milk whereby the tug of war between gods and demons causes the milky ocean to be thickened, and is turned into ambrosia. This is a symbol of the stirring of good and evil, which is eventually made into food for the soul. This tug of war or warring between good and evil has been an intricate philosophy in most religions. In Buddhism the wrathful deities hold the energies of good and evil.

The Christian Church adopted this pre-Christian goddess, Brigit, who worshipped the earth and all in it, and held that the animal kingdom were to be honoured as our friends and help mates. She was re-named Saint Brigid the nun, who founded her convent in Kildare (Gaelic for 'oak forest') in Ireland. The Christian fathers were very impressed with her many marvellous gifts, which included hand crafting of metal, looking after the dying, beautiful works of poetry, and courageous leadership. Though St. Brigid (also known as Brede, Bridget, and Bride) was a feisty woman of great inner strength and woman wisdom, in her so-called beatification the Goddess Brigit seems to have lost her own fiery somatic characteristics, and assumed those of the more acceptable nature of a sainted virgin nun.

What is the Cauldron?

The word 'cauldron' comes from the Celtic, *calla* or *caul*, or 'hood' – something encompassing the head of a child when born. This *call* or *caul* was said to hold the wisdom of all creation, and the child, whose head it covered, would never be lost at sea nor would her feet take her too far from home. It was a container, a safeguard, a protector of the spirit of the child. On a physical level, most dictionaries describe it as a large earthen or iron pot used for cooking over an open fire. It stands on three legs, and has a handle, and sometimes a lid. When a friend asked me, however, what the significance of the Cauldron was, I answered her thus: 'It symbolizes the container of all life, the feminine or earth soul, which holds all without judgement.'

The feminine face of divinity gathers everyone, and all, into her cloak of compassion and love. The Cauldron makes no judgement between day and night, birth and death, holy and profane, god and devil, good and bad, saint and sinner, creator and created, king and pauper etc. All is accepted within her deep expressive womb. Brigit's association with the Cauldron is important. Her all-embracing, non-judgemental acceptance of the whole of life, together with her deep and committed love for humanity, touches the soul of creation and the soul in us follows without knowing why. She is known as the 'keeper of the heart', which can be translated as 'keeper of the hearth', as 'hearth' and 'heart' are synonymous within the Celtic soul.

The flame of Brigit is symbolic of her passion, and the deep cleansing through fire that accompanies her work in our psyche. She is the brown, red-earthed divinity calling all people to live consciously from the centre of their own divine nature. In her mighty Cauldron, she stirs our earth-minds and Souls until we come out purified, and ready for service, to others and ourselves. Naturally, she doesn't discriminate because of gender; men who choose to live consciously in the world will undoubtedly be invited to experience her teachings in some form or other. She particularly calls on the male gender to come alive in her great soulful self. Her message to the male is: 'Your victories are no longer out there; they are flaming in the hearth of your own fire. Time to come home now to your soul. This be your victory.'

Having been taught by the Cauldron for the past eight years, I find that the teachings intensify as I do my own healing work. My questions change as I change. They spiral in me as I show a willingness to experience all of my precious life. Though they remain the same at the core, they also become more rounded, more life gathering as I do. A few months ago, when I was seeking help for some of the difficult questions regarding my life, it answered me thus: 'Seek not answers to these questions. Seek only to live each question fully, so that your life becomes the answer.'

This is the kind of ambivalence I have grown used to whenever I have asked for clarity or help. It is as though the rational mind alone is no longer the vehicle for knowing and understanding. Somehow, I have been able to stay with the questions long enough to experience them fully in my bones. The magick lies in being able to go to the cave of darkness (that quiet, dark place, where the reasoned mind knows to hush itself in the presence of an all-knowing other), and listen for the answers with the guts, blood, and tears of my own humanness. The Cauldron has shown me that I am totally equipped to heal all wounding of the past, and herein is holiness. I have had to make a very profound shift in consciousness regarding this word 'holy'. As I see it now, to be holy means to live fully in the world, which necessitates going beyond fear, to become more and more aware of my reactions to everything, and to heal my dysfunctioning patterns of relating.

Some time ago, I was in a group where we shared our definitions of saintliness. Mother Theresa, Gandhi, and Pope John XXIII were all named as examples of saints. My example was a woman of 46, living in a built-up area in Northern Ireland with little money to support her, and her five children. She cared for an elderly neighbour who was crippled with pain. Her sense of humour, and her willingness to go beyond the given in her life, and live each day to the full, encouraged me to be in the moment as much as possible. The man who was able to go to his neighbour, whom he had hated for years, and say 'Jim, I am sorry for the way I treated you, in actual fact I have been jealous of you all my life. I blamed you for the fact that you had money and I had not. I am sorry.' is another example of saint. When we can do courageous acts like this we become peacemakers and contribute to world peace. As a young person I was led to believe that saintliness was synonymous with self-inflicted physical pain, martyrdom, and miracle making. Most of the female saints were also virgins, as in young women who never experienced sex. There was something decisively holy about virginity, according to Catholic culture, which no doubt impressed us to maintain that position as long as possible.

The Cauldron teaches me that I am well informed. Questions themselves come from grace, and as such are holy and inspired. With this new consciousness, we go beyond our fears, thus widening soulfulness into embracing life more joyfully.

The sacred Cauldron

What the Cauldron represents is the womb of the Great Mother, representing male and female, yin and yang; waiting for the raw material of our natural emotions. She invites them to burn, to be stirred in her great container so that the heat of her fires may mix, boil, and bubble all the raw material of human anguish to form a great psychic stew for the hungry soul. This stew, this ambrosia, is necessary nourishment for the soul's welfare, without which it perishes for lack of passion, creativity, and real relationship with others. When we can risk this burning, this melting, we pass the initiation into the abundance of life. If we play safe and stay at the rim of the Cauldron, we will never experience the brand new breath of our own heart's song filling us with vitality and wellbeing. We need to dive into this great womb regardless of the fear, for she will keep beckoning anyway. Better to willingly succumb to her churning than to suffer the snuffed-out life of victim. The Cauldron speaks in symbols and so represents all language. It reveals itself in poetry, art, nature, music, dreams, sexuality, and dance etc. It is usually non-verbal in its revelations and can be understood only at a soul level. Therefore, it is important that the person seeking its wisdom understands the language of the soul.

The wisdom of the Cauldron is received through the medium of an open heart. Naturally, the great opener of the heart in the beginning is grief, and tears from the heart open wide the doors of communication. From this place wisdom of the Cauldron is welcomed. Later, joy and love open the heart wider so that more space is afforded for this wisdom to fill. The stirring of sorrow and joy, anger and peace, fear and love produce the Song of Songs, the great dance of renewal for the strengthening of the soul's journey to itself. Those who do not risk the splitting of their hearts stay fragmented rather than integrated, separate rather than at one with all life. They remain untouched and untouchable, therefore, unfeeling and withdrawn and fail to understand paradoxical living. Only those who have risked the melting of their own earth-minds in the womb of the Great Mother can truly feel safe to walk the world with grace and honour, laughter and song, for they understand living with paradox.

Teachings from the Cauldron

As the teachings of the Cauldron are not written in stone, it is not in the usual way of research that I share with you my findings. What I share with you, the reader is my experience of soul energy. Always I am challenged to be authentic, and the teachings show me the untilled land-scapes in me that need healing. If I am to teach 'the abundance of life', then I have to be willing to live it all. I ask you, the reader, to open your heart to the words, and if something in you calls you to listen more in depth, then do so. Do not forget of course, that you are being led by the great universal soul of humanity at this very important time in the evolution of our planet. This meeting may happen through your own belief system whether it is Christianity, Buddhism, Islam, or whatever. Ask for the help you need today to find your own treasures for your life within your own soul self.

Under the lid of the Cauldron

If the Cauldron has been a symbol of soul wisdom from past ages it has also been a symbol of ridicule, and a dishonouring of the true magick of the Great Mother archetype. It was always associated with witches in the past especially in Shakespeare's Macbeth where the three witches bubbled up all kind of trouble. So trouble, grotesqueness, and dark energy were linked to these older, isolated women. Therefore, the inquisition was acknowledged by the fathers of the church as an act of mercy to rid society of such evilness.

The bubbling is symbolic of the intensity with which the soul sets about her healing work in the psyches of human beings. We begin to feel her stirring of the unconscious nine tenths to the top of the pot.

We know when the stirring begins. We feel uncomfortable; we feel the churning of our unlived parts just below the surface. Something is calling for expression, and sometimes we do not know what it is. We just feel all stirred up. The churning of our unlived dreams, our unmet passion, our cries for good parenting, even though we have reached fifty years of age is all part of our awakening. It may be that a relationship goes wrong, and we feel lonely inside, bereft, and unsafe in the world. We become more conscious of our hurt parts. If we look further we see the unhealed patterns of early childhood. The Cauldron is heating up slowly, and slowly our awareness takes us deeper into unknown territory, and we need help. We can at any time refuse to look at what is being brought to the surface. We can say no at any time. We will not have to look at, smell, or taste anything we do not feel ready for. But she will persist; she will stir gently under a warm heat until you at last realize that you have to begin to own the ingredients, smell them, feel them and taste them.

When you deal with the stuff directly under the surface you can then feel her stirring more deeply with her big ladle. The sour taste of your unhealed parts, when mixed with the clear soup of compassion, and love for yourself, results in a deeper understanding, and acceptance of your unclaimed soulfulness. As you work with her, the soul within, deeper and deeper she will go until she is scraping the bottom of the pot. As you look back on the great healing in your life, you will begin to give thanks for the wisdom of her stirring in you, and you will honour your own integrity, more and more.

Humanistic psychology teaches that we project onto others any trait or attribute we do not like in ourselves. This is the big lesson from the Cauldron for this age. It is not easy for me to own my own arrogance, so I put it out there onto my partner. Now I feel instantly relieved, for he is the arrogant one, and I am the long-suffering angel. I do not own my intolerance, so the local government is a likely candidate for my projection. It is clear that Hitler was a brute, and an abuser, and the same goes for Stalin, and Saddam Hussein. This is well documented. Therefore, I do not have to look at my intolerance, or my internal abuser, or my internal murderer as long as I can find acceptable and well-known candidates out there for them. Naturally, I have not killed another, nor have I with full knowledge, abused another. However, I have learned the more subtle forms of abuse, intolerance, and arrogance, out of which I can operate when I am not conscious.

In my marriage, I was the good girl, very friendly, and outgoing. My husband was of a quiet disposition, and my extroversion, so-called, was in direct contrast to his so-called introversion. In a relationship, when one partner does not express her/his feelings, the other over-compensates (unconsciously), and has double feelings to cope with. My relationship was such. Also, it is also difficult to have two stars in a relationship if they have not done their healing work. My relationship was such. I had to be the star, the shining one, the angel. So where did my projected part, the devil, go? My poor husband played the role well for many years. I hope that I have

FINDHORN Press

Tel 01309 690582 / Freephone 0800 389 9395
Fax 01309 690036
e-mail info@findhornpress.com
www.findhornpress.com

Thank you for choosing this book. We appreciate your interest and support.

If you would like to receive our full catalogue of books card sets and cds, please fill in this card and mail it to us.

❏ Please send Findhorn Press latest catalogue

❏ Please send information about the Findhorn Foundation in Scotland

In which book did you find this card? _____

Where did you buy this book? _____

Please write
your name and
address here
(please PRINT)

}

What is your email address? _____

<u>*to:*</u>

FINDHORN PRESS

305a The Park, Findhorn
Forres IV36 3TE
Scotland, UK

learned to call back some more of my misplaced parts. I want to be a holy woman, with all of me owned in me. Only then can I heal them.

Why was it so difficult for me to own my arrogance and pride? The Cauldron teaches that most people live in fear, and so cannot live the abundance of life. It comforts us in the words: 'Take your fears as you would a small trembling child, and warm them at the hearth of your loving kindness.'

My fear was that of being rejected. If I had been angry or arrogant as a child, I would have been abandoned not only by my parents but by God who did not like angry children. Therefore, I learned very quickly to be good, and loving, and not to have needs. This fear of life followed me for a long time, and it was responsible for many of my choices.

When I was a nun in the 1960s, we all worked together, prayed together, and ate together. The emphasis was on losing oneself. I learned how to be holy by hating myself. I repressed any so-called negative feelings by abusing my body, and calling it spiritual practice. With self-abandonment I offered my young unlived life to God. This I did because I loved Jesus and wanted to serve him for the rest of my life. Had I been conscious I would have realized that I became a nun because I was afraid to live 'in the world of sin'. I was so afraid to express who I was, the whole of me, that I chose the 'great escape'. I was afraid of my sexuality having been told from childhood that it was dangerous. It was easier to opt for denial of myself as a woman than to look at the origin of my dysfunctioning. I handed over all responsibility and power for my life. Fear of life drove me to self-rejection. The very thing I was afraid of experiencing from others.

I had fear bubbling under the lid of the Cauldron: fear of offending Jesus; so I went out of my body in long meditations, and prayer. My earth-mind really protected me from breaking my heart. I did not notice the transforming of this young girl into a 'good' nun, and a so-called 'holy woman of God'. How could the wisdom of the Cauldron have helped me to see the way I was cheating on my own life, and therefore, was not of legitimate help to others?

Clearly, the mother superior of the order might have delved deeper to question my unconscious motives for joining her community of nuns. In those days 'for the love of God' was sufficient reason. Many ex-nuns, with whom I worked later as a counsellor, realized that there had been incest in their childhood, and the convent offered refuge. The shame you carry prevents you from being fully in life, and so for many the silence of the nunnery appealed to them. Many women had suffered broken relationships and chose Jesus on the rebound. This aspect of being a nun appealed to me. I did not have to have sex with Jesus, and he loved me all the same. I also wore his ring, and carried the image of my spouse hanging on a cross around my neck.

Many young women like me had been abused by the Catholic religion that insisted on our evilness: that all women were intrinsically temptresses. This theology was also in a very subtle way, abusive to men. It suggested that they were ruled by their sexual urges only and unable to control them and regarded them as no better than the animal with its basic impulses, and instincts. My entering the convent was a reaction to life in my body. When we simply react, we are not acting consciously. According to the Cauldron, the great challenge to us in these times is to live more and more consciously in our bodies.

Under the lid of the Cauldron also lay my childhood patterns of caretaking everyone. Guilt and shame would have been stirring around also, creating havoc. With the help of a good psycho-spiritual guide I would have been able to look at these patterns, and heal them. I would have seen the reasons behind the choices I made.

The teachings tell us that we are not alone, that help and guidance are always with us in the form of the seen and unseen; but we want to be in control. Loss of control means the earth-mind has to surrender. Seemingly, we are offered symbolically three chances to get back on course. The soul uses the unskillful choices of the earth-mind as grist for the mill of healing.

Having embarked on my own healing work, and having got to the stage where I was able to see the abusers, not as evil people, but as wounded, and unhealed, I was able to feel compassion for them, as well as for myself. Clearly, I see now that everything that I chose from the unskillful places of earth-mind had painful consequences. Now they are part of my blessings.

The Cauldron taught me that I had to look at the way in which, because of fear, I subtly manipulated others, and controlled many situations. How many times I had imposed on others to have my will done as I was afraid of failure. Aah! The compassion it takes to see our own fragility, and love it back into the soul of us again. The Cauldron teaches that we need to be able to 'see our own faces in the face of all humanity', only this way can we become truly holy.

Healing our lives takes a long time, indeed lifetimes. But it becomes easier to see the patterns emerge from the darkness.

Seven moons of healing

The Cauldron teaches that there are 'seven moons of healing'. The following are the stages or *aite,* which is Gaelic for 'places':

1. Entering the cave of darkness
2. Touching the bones of the broken woman/man
3. Telling the stories *(scealta)*
4. Singing the soul of compassion
5. Calling the prodigal
6. Sharing the gifts
7. Re-entering the cave

1. Entering the cave of darkness

When we enter the cave of darkness, we begin a journey that is spiralling upwards. The way is not linear as in having a clearly defined starting and ending point, nor is it circular as in 'going round in circles', revisiting the same old places of dysfunctioning. Most of us do not enter the cave voluntary. Our soul, of course, uses every occasion birthed from choices of our earth-mind to guide us to the mouth of the cave. The Irish have a saying: 'If you do not go to hell yourself, the devil will pull you in by the heels.' There is some truth in this, though I like to think that it is not the devil that takes you to so-called hell, but your wise soul who shows you where your hell is. For many, going voluntarily to the cave seems like self-punishment because they are not aware of their reactions to stressful living. When someone suggests to us we might look at why we are dysfunctioning in life, we react in anger. Fear advises us to 'stay with the known'; therefore, we use every means possible to stay outside the cave.

In my work with the dying, I have encountered so many people who find it difficult to accept death as a fact of life. Death is the boogey man because we have never been educated in its mysteries. The whole idea of letting go is too painful. We invest so much of our happiness in others, so that when they are dying, our whole lives are shattered. The cave experience urges us to look at this grief. What we really need is to have some loving, non-judgemental other to witness our grief, and help us to open our hearts into mercy for our grieving selves. Feelings like anger, fear, jealousy, depression, hopelessness, and denial need to be expressed through the body. We are asked to experience our losses fully instead of distracting ourselves and ignoring them. These words from one of my songs encourage us to:

> *Dance in the shadows till you hear*
> *The sound of your feet upon the ground.*
> *Dance in the shadows till the fear inside you*
> *Breaks your silence with its healing ancient sound.*

How can fear have a healing sound? The natural sound of fear is a scream. In my work I have helped people to express their fears through sound, which eventually becomes music. The hymn 'Amazing Grace' advises that it is grace itself that shows us our fears and indeed grace releases them. J. Newton (1725-1807).

2. Touching the bones of the broken woman/man

One man admitted to me some time ago, that his fear of the cave was about his fear of the dark; and his fear of the dark was about his fear of his own emotions, which he had kept hidden. His messages from childhood were that emotions had to be controlled or else they would take over. (Emotion suggests a movement.) The reverse would seem to be true: our own dysfunctional feelings find expression in inappropriate ways. Suppression needs expression because many times this manifests as illness or accidents, or even heart attacks.

This dialogue, which I had with a prisoner in one of the Scottish jails, will demonstrate the tragedy of repressed and suppressed feelings.

Phyllida: 'Why did you kill your wife, John?' (Not his real name)

John: 'Because she always went on, and on at me.'

Phyllida: 'What did she go on about?'

John: 'Everything, like I'm no good, I never do anything right, that kind of stuff.'

Phyllida: 'Who else used to go on at you?'

John: 'My mother never quit at me, always nagging me all my life.'

Phyllida: 'Anyone else?'

John: 'My teacher too, never got anything right. She was a right b…'

Phyllida: 'Do you have regrets about killing your wife?'

John: 'Aye, I do, you see, I killed the wrong woman, didn't I?'

He was not laughing. He realized the pain started long before he met his wife. She was a reminder of his mother. Had John been given the opportunity to do some healing work on his mother and teacher, I wonder if he would have killed his wife. This does not ever excuse murder, or any form of abuse; it is a psychological reason why some people kill. Some, and certainly not all people, have to find victims to persecute in order to relieve their own pain, to feel powerful in themselves. Elisabeth Kübler-Ross MD believed that we all have a 'Hitler' inside, and we are all capable of violent deeds should we be put to the test. She added we also have a 'Mother Teresa' inside.

3. Telling of the stories (*scealta*)

This is such an important ingredient in the healing process. We Irish have a great love for a good story. We delight in telling the stories of Fionn McCull and his band of warriors, or the misdeeds of evil elves and goblins. (It is more difficult to hear the stories of contemporary evil in our once 'Isle of saints and scholars'.) When our stories are witnessed and honoured, in a group of compassionate listeners, healing flows into all the hurt places and we are vindicated. As Celts, we believe that the telling of the stories of our ancestors has immediate healing effect on the living, and the dead. I believe that 'in the telling of the father's story, the son does not have to live it', has much truth to it. When the father's story is not known, the psyche of the son picks it up, and tries to finish it. The same is true for the mother and daughter. So many young people have to live out their parent's unmet dreams. A verse in one of my song advises:

> *You know young man you won't heal alone,*
> *You've got your mother and your father stuck to your bones.*
> — *Phyllida and Healing Voices C.D Touched 2003* [iv]

4. Singing the soul of compassion

This is something we have never been taught to do. The Cauldron teaches us how to sing our soul song of love to ourselves. It tells us when we can take compassion on our own brokenness that we look in through the eye of love on our own suffering. This look of love is filled with grace and blessings, and this is what heals us. As long as we condemn ourselves, and carry the guilt of our past, we cannot be healed. How can we possibly heal with such destructive bedfellows? If we could but know our innocence, we would immediately fall into love with ourselves, and healing would be immediate. But old messages remain a long time in the psyche, long after the messengers have gone. Obsessing about our past mistaches, and bad choices, is a subtle form of self-abuse. We will not allow ourselves to have peace of mind or heart. It is as if the script says: 'You are guilty, and I will keep on reminding you of this'. Learning to look at our obsessive patterns, with loving kindness, helps us to deal with them, and eventually heal them. This is the message of the Cauldron.

5. Calling the prodigal or lost parts

This is only possible when we have already taken compassion on ourselves, and have touched our brokenness. So many people call home their projections and then feel guilty for having projected in the first place! If you are still feeling guilty or ashamed, this is not the time to do this exercise. You will do it only because you want to be 'good', and do the 'right' thing. So-called premature forgiveness, letting go of blame, does not last because it does not have the self-love to back it up; it comes from fear. You need to look at why you call back your lost parts. You do so from a deep knowing that I am that which I name in others, and I want to be a whole person with all my erring parts called home to my heart. In this way they can be healed. Remember, there is a time for all things under heaven. Your timing is important.

In Buddhism, the teaching of karma suggests that whatever I create returns to me. It is both impersonal and personal. All symptoms are karmic, and these symptoms are messages about disharmony, about incongruence. In actual fact, the universe returns to us what we have activated figuratively in the world. It is the doctrine of 'what we reap, we sow'. In Buddhism also, we have the symbols of the begging bowls, whereby, the monk, or renunciate goes into the village with an empty bowl, and humbly waits for it to be filled by others. This filling of his bowl symbolically returns to him what he has first given out. Our Celtic ancestors used the bowl symbolically. It represented our lived and yet-to-be lived lives. We come into the world ready to continue our story, to fill the bowl, the Cauldron again. The emptying happens at that transformation called death, whereby, the great life force receives our bowl, overflowing with mystery, empties it, reviews the experiences of this life, in relation to the other lives we have lived, and with the same bowl we travel back to earth, ready to fill it again. Naturally, I call this bowl, soul. Soul is a word not used in Buddhism. It had to wait until the Christ came so that we could fully understand it. John Tarrant, a Buddhist teacher and author, speaks of emotional healing work, soul work, as apart from the experience of mediation practice.

6. Sharing the gifts

This is where the creative and sharing self delights in its own soulfulness. When I have touched the depths of my own wilderness, I come home laden with the gifts. These gifts uncover my own joy and add to the joy of others. I am always surprised at the various gifts of creativity that have been hidden in people's psyches. Seemingly, only when we face our shadows, and begin to love ourselves are the gifts uncovered. People are surprised when this happens. Their creative juices were so hidden under the dross that they did not know of their existence. It is the earth-mind that keeps us small, keeps us embarrassed, and keeps us isolated.

I notice when I give a concert, I am still a little nervous before it starts. Once I go on the stage, and look into the eyes of the people there, all nervousness leaves me. I am in the company of friends. The beloved between us is in charge. I am simply the mouthpiece, and I have no fear of not getting it right. There is no so-called 'right' or 'wrong', where love is concerned. There is only love.

7. Re-entering the cave

This is not to be mistaken for visiting the cave for the first time. Remember, we are never back to the beginning again regarding our healing work. We re-enter more enlightened, in order to clear off any surface suppressed feelings. It will never be as dark again. It is important that we do this seventh stage even though we feel there is nothing to clear. It is a good practice simply to retreat every six months or so in order to be with our own energy, and creativity. Brigit talks of: 'the need for gathering ourselves in'. I believe this 'gathering in' is a necessary part of healing. The more clarity we get from our time in the cave, the more conscious we become. I look forward to the time when we will all just share our gifts of peace and love together with no need for re-entering the cave. Until then however, I am willing to keep re-entering it to find treasures.

Celtic Wombman

Celtic woman was sensitive to poetry and philosophy. She had strength which came not from muscle, though she was also very fit, but from a deep sense of her own internal authority. When she performed ritual, men stood in awe at her dignity and obeyed her authority, which was not to oppress but to build up. She knew she represented the goddess, *Dearcú,* (Red Hound). She represented swiftness, strength, loyalty, knowing, guarding, passion, and the ability to smell danger. She regarded all forms of life as sacred. Her magick was her strength, which could be used to destroy or to heal. Her menstrual blood fertilized the land. It was also for the anointing of young women who were faced with the demons of self-destruction, suicide. It was said to help bring them back to their bloodline.

Babies were also fed the placenta, and women of childbearing age also partook of it to aid their fertility. They burned the dead with elaborate ceremony of singing, howling, and dancing, and had their bodies painted. Celtic women loved jewellery, hair dying, arm bracelets, anklet adornments, and garment dying. They often used hair dying to confuse their men!! They were very emotional and passionate and sexuality was expressed in sacred rites of passage. At times of ritual they showed great discipline and obedience to the priestess.

They were of gypsy personality and loved to roam feeling the need to uproot from time to time to broaden their horizons. It was said of Deirdre of the sorrows, Celtic goddess of the grieving woman, that her fierceness was as powerful as were her tears of passion, and sorrow, and her sorrow was the child of joy she carried with her. This suggests the paradoxical world in which our female ancestors lived.

Living paradox

Celtic women realized that Wombman not only experiences life on earth, she is also the life which she experiences. She is not separate from life within the experience. She is also the antithesis of her experience, in so far as she can detach, and remain separate. Wombman is the giver of life and is the life she creates. She is also the destroyer. She is willing to be destroyed in the act of creation itself.

When Wombman grieves, she is not separate from the act of grieving, nor is she detached from that which she mourns. When Wombman mourns her lost loves, her youth, her unfulfilled dreams, she is both the act of mourning and the subject/object of her grief. So Wombman is said not only to be the subject of her experience of life, but the object she experiences also. She not only creates the very experience, she is the experience and life living it.

When Wombman rejoices at the dance of life, she is at the same time, albeit unconsciously, grieving its laments. When she is singing a song of love and passion, she is at the same time, howling her loveless and sad passionless life. Her act of separateness creates space for the one to predominate over the other – still the paradox remains. Since all creation flows from her vast womb, she is the first cause of all life. She is also the last. She is the sacred void, the place of non-conceptual knowing. When the refinement of human form is complete she will be both the refiner, and that which is refined.

Wombman is said to be 'in the heart of all creation'. This is true and false, for she is the very heart itself: that place of pure emptiness out of which all worlds are created; therefore, she is not just in creation, but is creation. Not only is her voice sounding on the waters, she is the waves. Not only does she mourn the loss of her children on earth, she is the very act of mourning, as well as the children she mourns. Wombman knows by nature that life is impermanent yet everlasting, transient yet fully now, continuously dying and always in life.

Wombman is both the subject of her love, and the act of loving itself. Therefore, she cannot but truly feel with extremes. Her emotionality is deeper and more immediate than man's emotionality. The moon and her monthly cycles affect her. At the time of the fullness of the moon Wombman is said to experience madness, according to what is determined 'normal', which is not always 'natural'. It is said that at this time, Wombman is more in touch with her non-dual nature and her paradoxical experiences of life.

Celtic man

It is written of Celtic man that he was war hungry, and spent his time fighting battles. In Heuneburg and Hochdorf in Germany, there is rich evidence of perhaps the first Celtic settlers in Europe. Archaeologists have found there that Celtic man was a skillful craftsman who built his own home in a circular fashion, (awareness of the feminine), painted it white to reflect the sun, (male aspect), and sparsely decorated it inside. They were hard-working farmers who tended the land and cattle, and worked alongside nature. There is evidence also of Greek craftsmanship in the beautiful ornate torcs, swords, and jewellery, and they made their own ornate chariots, which were later buried with them.

Their trade with Greece helped develop their own skills in pottery and ironwork. It has been suggested that the word Celt itself came from Greece. It was a way of describing a culture rather than a tribe. At Hochdorf a golden torc and sword were found seemingly belonging to a chieftain. The Iron Age made Celts very rich. Through this medium their creative skills were openly displayed. They also spoke Latin and Greek. This aspect of Celtic man still flourished in Ireland during the time of 'the persecutions' when education was denied and teachers and scholars taught in the hedgerows and ditches whilst someone kept watch.

Where does biological man find his essence? Initially a boy child finds his identity with his mother. Her approval is everything otherwise his feelings of worthiness are at stake. A man's wisdom draws itself from a different well to that of women, albeit, no less powerful or full of creative gifts.

Celtic wise men (shamans) used their own phlegm (as did Peruvian shamans) as a potent container for the handing down of wisdom. They believed that liquids from the body hold medicinal attributes of life force, that when gifted is a passing on of one's creative life juices. In the West when we spit at a person it is seen as an act of aggression, but in the times of pre-Christian Ireland, spitting was known as sending a gift to the earth. Some of the gypsies in Ireland still hold a ceremony of mixing the urine from a betrothed couple on the morning of their wedding. This was a mixing of the tribes and an acceptance of each other's tribe. The combined urine was then poured into the earth as a blessing.

Man expresses his life less emotionally, and more conceptually than woman. This is natural for him. However, when he suppresses his emotions out of fear then his dysfunctioning, like that of the woman, affects his wellbeing. It is very difficult for modern man to find his own source, his own rich fertile place of maleness. In the workplace he is being replaced by automation, in the home he is being replaced by childminders, and in his interactions with his peers his success rate in the world is being judged by his possessions. Men in this time find it difficult to know how to be in the earth. One man confided in me some months ago 'Phyllida, I don't know how to be in the world any more. If I am too manly, I am called butch or chauvinist. If I am too feminine, I am called soft, and women don't want that. How do I behave as a man who is seen as loving, yet at times also angry, confused yet also determined? I don't know'.

My answer to him was in the form of a questionnaire:

1. What is maleness?
2. How do you define your own gender beginning with the statement 'All men are ...?'
3. What are your fears around your own gender?
4. What are your fears around feelings?
5. What are your beliefs about your own sense of responsibility?
6. How was your relationship with your father?
7. How was your relationship with your mother?
8. How have you had to change your ways in order to be accepted by others?
9. Continue this statement 'All women are...'
10. What do you do to be loved?
11. Define 'success'.

Having considered these questions at home alone he phoned me, and said he wanted to share the answers. We met some time later, and he shared with me his difficulties of being with himself, and consequently being with others. His father's strict, controlling ways that suggested that a woman's place was in the home, and a man's place was to take control no longer worked. His girlfriend's insistence that he share all his feelings did not seem right to him, as he did not feel as deeply as she did about different issues. When he opened the door for his girlfriend on entering a room she told him she could open it herself, and what was he looking for, sex?

When he once admired another woman for her strength and power, his girlfriend suggested that he did not love her because of her weakness. He felt that women think that all men want is sex and that women needed to know that all men want is to be loved, just as that is all they want. Men go about it in different ways, and everyone is here to share with each other their difficulties, and their differences, and to heal. Women don't know any more what they want from men and this is very confusing for both sexes. He then added that his mother never really believed in him; she kept him dependent on her for a long time.

Celtic man, like Wombman learned from nature. From her he learned about inner strength, about boundaries, about self-discipline, and the protection of the young. Celtic man was also a poet, creative even in his wars, and respect for his opponent was as important as the sword with which he killed him. He shape shifted into the animal he hunted and used their qualities in his fighting. He was so in touch with his own animnal self that there was no separation between him and the outer animal. Honouring of oneself was innate; therefore, honouring of all creation was natural. He did not have to contend with the sedentary life that men live today, nor did he have to contend with the stress of financial worries due to lack of employment. Role identity gave both security and acknowledgement to both men and women, therefore, children were less confused within the home, and role modelling was secure.

The great gods of the Celtic world, like *Lugh* and *Cú Cúchlainn*, were imbued with strength, wisdom, and discipline, and Celtic man was in direct relationship with their energies. The role of father in the life of *Lugh* as he protected his son *Cú Cúchlainn* whilst the latter slept his dreamless sleep, or as could be described as in deep meditation, was to guard the son from bodily harm. *Lugh* guarded the male population with his wisdom of initiator into other world realities. This journeying was to gather truths, and bring them back to share with their tribe.

The gods were the caretakers of the tribes, and Celtic man had a deep responsibility to transmit tribal values and norms to the younger generations so that customs, rituals, and ceremonies could be continued. Celtic man loved drama and dance, and before hunting for food he would paint his body, do his sun dance, and call upon his ancestors to assist, then with the blessing of the oldest man in his tribe go and kill an animal. This ritual was done as a natural exchange to the animal kingdom as he himself would offer to the animals his own body at death. Ordinary people had a choice whether to have their bodies put into the ground where the animal life could partake of it, or later to be burnt. Higher ranking people were buried with their chariots and earth belongings.

Chapter 3

Natural versus Dysfunctioning Emotions

Natural emotions and their functions/dysfunctions

Elisabeth Kübler-Ross MD taught that there are only five natural feelings or emotions, anger, fear, love, jealousy, and grief. These emotions are often distorted by our conditioned living. I also include sexuality as a natural emotion. I also have a belief that we carry unfinished dysfunctioning patterns of relating from incarnation to incarnation.

Celtic Consciousness teaches that we carry destructive emotional energies from our parents and ancestors, and as we heal they also heal. Indeed they believed that whatever we do on earth plane affects all created phenemona. Whilst it is very important that we find spaces, healing ways to express our unacceptable emotions, I stress time and time again that we need not revisit their original birthplaces – childhood. We do not need to bleed the scabs once they have formed! Many people traumatize themselves over and over by reminding themselves of their unhappy, and indeed, abusive childhoods by digging up the past, blaming others, pointing fingers, and constantly robbing the grave by digging up the carcass. This is a means of keeping one a victim, and never seeing the light of day of one's own inner authority and responsibility as an adult. It is tiring for others having to listen to our 'gossiping' about ourselves in order to receive love or attention. Once we have healed we need not squeeze the wound open again.

Natural versus Dysfunctioning Emotions

Natural	Function	Dysfunction
Anger	Helps us to have our needs met and say not to what does not serve us or society.	Rage, violence, aggression, passive aggression, frustration, cynicism, sarcasm, gossiping, criticizing, threatening another, belittling.
Fear	Shows us where to be cautious, shows us our insecurities, fight or fight response; only two natural fears: 1. loud noise from behind. 2. falling from a height.	Phobias, neurosis, obsessiveness, defensiveness.
Love	Sharing our lives, feelings of wellbeing, outreach to others. Sharing our creativity. Confidence in who we are.	Possessiveness, conditional – I love you if, control over, codependency, sentimentality.
Jealousy	Shows us what we want and who we want to emulate,	Envy, projected possessiveness, I'll show them 'me too' syndrome.
Grief	Helps us share tears of loss and express our feelings, brings us out of isolation, transforming, expressed love, telling the story.	Inertia, detachment, leaking tears, inappropriate dependence on loved ones who died, stuckness, overworks, numbness, confusion, nostalgia, inappropriate guilt.

Sexuality	Experiencing body in a sexual way, respects boundaries, expression procreation, beyond conceptual thinking.	Rape, leaking sensuality, pornography, reference to a child's growing bodyshape, of spirituality, cult abuse, inappropriate touching, sex as punishment, addiction to orgasms.

At Kübler-Ross workshops, a safe sacred place was provided for people to express the fears, tears, and rages of childhood that had clogged up their whole emotional system. No doubt that was just the beginning of the journey to the centre of themselves. I believe that my deepest meditations were when I sat with people, helping them get in touch with their rage, to out it into their grief, and fears, and eventually dance their joy into letting go of the perpetrators, and therefore, be forgiven. This for me was a holy time, a time when I enabled others as I had been enabled myself to risk going into the hell of their pain, to touch their own madness, and experience their own joy. Elisabeth maintained that therapists can only take their clients as far as they had gone themselves. She was not happy when people tried to escape their pain through positive thinking and unrealistic affirmations. This time of watching, truly being present whilst another goes into their hell, and eventually transcends it into a place of self-acceptance, true compassion, and outreach to others, was for me experiencing the brokenness, and the healing all in one. I never worked alone. For me the beloved, the oversoul watched with us, and all so-called negative energy expressed was transformed, was changed by the great alchemist herself 'love'. We did not have to do relaxation therapy with these people. We did not have to teach them meditation. We did not have to tell them what compassion was; they experienced it. Our singing and dancing, our true laughter and outreach were signs that transformation had happened, and this transformation would continue.

In Buddhism rage is seen as an unskillful way of interacting, and is judged as being an inferior way of being. Yes, rage is a very unskillful way of relating to others. Blocked, accumulative anger becomes rage, and from there we commit terrible atrocities, both with others and ourselves. I have experienced rage terrorize a community in Northern Ireland and have been at the receiving end of its outbursts. Self-rage often ends in suicide and/or murder. Some Buddhist masters maintain that to out the angry emotions is to pollute the earth. Whilst we hold and suppress our so-called negative feelings, we are not only polluting ourselves but are negatively affecting the universe.

The great oversoul transforms all expressed emotions into love. Our singing and dancing, our joy and love for one another at such gatherings are proof already of this. Any judgement of our feelings is a judgement and to seek happiness at the expense of dealing with our childhood rage is futile. In the convent I meditated all day long, it did not help me find exuberance and joy in life. Only when I was allowed to express the fears from childhood in a loving all-embracing environment, where unconditional acceptance allowed me to share my rage, could I experience the joy already waiting to be uncovered.

Whilst we will not look at the six emotions in depth, I feel it is important to talk about blocked anger, and how natural anger, when appropriately expressed, can help both ourselves and others.

Anger

Having worked in two prisons in the United Kingdom, I realized that most of the men I worked with had been victims at a very early age, and found their own victims later on. As I mentioned before, this is not to excuse violence but it is a psychological reason for acts of such unconsciousness in our society.

Natural anger takes about 15 seconds according to Elisabeth Kübler-Ross MD. Natural anger is simply saying 'no'. It is that inner authority that knows what serves us, and what does not. It does not have a charge. Natural anger is not loud, it is not violent, and it is not shouting or aggressive. It is the adult in us stating his/her needs and wants clearly. When our needs were not met as children, we often cried to draw attention to this fact, a natural expression of grief. Often the young child goes into a temper tantrum to get further attention. The child who can express natural anger and get positive attention, will naturally do better than the one who is shut up, smacked, and beaten because their natural need for expression is unacceptable. Many children who are not allowed to express natural anger, take it out on small animals, or by being passively aggressive, get their own revenge on the adult. I have a story about this.

My friend, Hannah, was unable to own a 'no', or to be heard, so she acted out her aggression in the way that only a child could do. She wandered around the neighbourhood, with a bucket asking everyone for their caterpillars. Having collected a bucket load, she would take them back to her own garden, and carefully put them on her father's brussel sprout plants. Such power! A sense of justified revenge came from every munch of the caterpillar on the growing plant.

Was your 'no' listened to as a child? Did you have to have a temper tantrum in order to have your needs met, or did you also have recourse to passive aggression? Passive aggression is no longer natural anger being expressed, but the accumulation of frustration. Remember that a child's needs are often quite different from what they want. Love also can say no at these times.

To bring healing to our dysfunctioning anger, i.e. anger with a charge – which is actually rage, it is advisable to practise the opposite once we have done the initial expressing in a therapeutic setting. By practising the opposite I am then in charge, not the dysfunctioning feeling. Being an impatient person, I need to practise patience so I might set one day apart, and in my morning quiet time I might promise myself 'today I will attract situations whereby I will learn patience'. I then ask the help of my soul. If I am being arrogant I will seek out situations whereby loving kindness can cancel out that arrogance. If I tell a lie, naturally I will go to the person and confess, and in the same day ask that I might attract a situation whereby I will tell the whole truth. Doing these practices I am helping my earth-mind to accept another reality other than the conditioned one. Becoming conscious of dysfunctional feelings, and when they are about to erupt, is indeed halfway to healing them.

Grief

What is grief for? Where does it come from? How helpful is it? How best can we deal with it?

We will not attempt to answer all these questions, for each is a chapter on its own, and there are many books written on grief. They are simply questions on which to ponder with an open heart, and new and fresh mind.

In my book *A Celtic Book of Dying*[v] I refer to the six stages of healing grief. These are denial, bargaining, anger, depression, acceptance, and surrender. Many people think that surrender is passive, accepting, or giving up. For me surrender means to go beyond faith, hope and trust, and with the assurance of the soul let go, and be led. It is my belief that fear often masks itself in the form of hope and trust, which seek an outcome; a goal to be reached. Surrender is the movement that lets go of all into the guidance of the soul alone.

These stages mentioned above are not chronological, but can be visited at any time during active grieving. It does not mean that the grieving is non-progressive. It simply means that there is a time for all stages, and each stage is a transformation in itself.

The old Irish adage 'tears that are not shed become the well of grief, in which most of us drown' suggests that tears are healing, and tears that are not shed overwhelm us, and in this overwhelming we drown. A drowning person cannot feel the earth beneath their feet. A drowning person cannot be fully in life. A drowning person is controlled by fear, which prevents him from feeling anything but annihilation. The sharing of our tears is a natural human act, which when not allowed expression alienates us, makes us less than human, and we hide into our own worlds where joy is *canadh a bfuil caillte ionam* – 'a song that is lost in me'. When we are unable to actively grieve our losses, be they the loss of a loved one, or separation from something in our lives that was meaningful to us, we enter into what I call inactive or unexpressed grief.

When did we as human beings learn to suppress our grief?

For many it started in childhood. A young child is not embarrassed about her emotions, nor is she worried about being heard having them. The embarrassment and anxiety around expressing feelings comes when she has learned that certain feelings are not acceptable in her household. I clearly remember that sad or angry emotions were not acceptable in my family, and anger was seen as sinful. We were told 'stop crying, or you will get something to cry about'. Later, at school, we were told that God was an angry God, and Jesus wept at the grave of Lazareth. We were also commanded to fear the Lord, but not allowed to fear the dark. God was allowed to be angry. God was allowed to be jealous. Jesus was allowed his tears, and to be angry, but I was five years old, my tears were unacceptable, my fear of the dark unacceptable, my anger was unacceptable. This was very confusing to say the least of it. I used to spend hours contemplating all of this in the space under the stairs. No wonder I found it difficult to understand the complex world of adults.

Men and grief

Often at workshops, I find that men express their grief with difficulty. They have been told for years that 'real men do not cry', so they literally tighten up, and deny their own softness. Men have had to harden their hearts in order to survive, in order to serve their country as soldiers. Many men find refuge in a bottle, in sex, in overworking, in overachieving, when the grief is too hard to bear. Often men cry when they drink as it uninhibits them so they have access to their feelings. This kind of expression whilst at least allows the tears to well up in the eyes often leads to melancholy and regret. Shame sets in later when they realize 'what they have done' under the influence of alcohol. Many men also find it difficult to express their anger or to confront especially if at home parents had argued. Early childhood conditioning makes them revert to being frightened children.

Guilt

What is it? When did we learn guilt? How helpful is it? How best can we deal with it?

In Celtic times, when one was found guilty of transgressing the Breton laws in Ireland, the elders gathered with the Druids around the oak tree, and held court to decide the outcome. There was a hierarchy of wrongdoing, and also a hierarchy of punishment for same. To curse another, or to call on the gods to harm another, or to create spells that would leave another disabled, were all punishable by the loss of a limb, by the forfeiting of assets, or by public disgrace. The guilty one, having endured their punishment, was then allowed back into society, and carried on as usual. Appropriate guilt was seen to be felt, therefore, the *tuatha*, or 'tribe' was satisfied.

Guilt is a feeling we have when we have wronged another. This is a natural self-monitoring emotion. Appropriate guilt helps us to interact with each other, with love and compassion instead of either disempowering or abusing others. Inappropriate guilt has great power to lower self-esteem, whereby, we punish ourselves for seeming wrong-doing. It robs us of self-love, and keeps us in our own prison. It holds the threat 'if they only knew what you are like, how bad you are', over us until we truly believe our own condemnations. It is the non-forgiving of ourselves, the self-abandonment that isolates us from others. It is the unwanted baggage we willingly carry as victims. For the rest of this section please read guilt as inappropriate guilt.

When did we learn this guilt? When we are small, we acquire our sense of self from the adults around us, namely: parents, teachers, church ministers, and later from our peers. If we grew up in an atmosphere of criticism, never getting it right, always having to be there for others, never having our needs met, then we are emotionally crippled. Later on, we internalize the voices and messages, and begin to believe we are not good enough. If God was held as one who judged us for the least misdemeanor, who saw and criticized our every move, then we criticize and judge our own actions, and condemn ourselves before someone else can.

According to my friend Eolath MaGee who died July 2005, the

internal judge has three distinct attributes, which may be expressed in the following way:

1. Knows all things – everybody knows you are no good,
    you are wrong, what else can be expected from you.
2. Can predict the future – mark my words you'll pay for this,
    you'll never get it right.
3. Is always right – you should have done so and so,
    you ought to know better, it's your fault.

My own sense of guilt that I carried for years came from religious abuse. Having been told at the age of five that I was responsible for the death of poor Jesus left me with a burden of shame that only they who have suffered abuse as children can truly understand.

How helpful is guilt? The only question you have to ask yourself regarding guilt is 'Is this voice/message, helping me right now regarding this situation?' If it is not then it is purely negative and is not a healing force in your life. When did you first hear these messages? Who told you, you were unworthy? Who told you, you were no good, you were stupid, unloving? The internal judge goes back a long way. Go back and find him, and talk to him. You'll find that the result of this conversation will be that you will touch your righteous anger because it is the flip side of inappropriate guilt. Anger has energy. Guilt is depressive, servile, and stagnant.

How to deal with guilt: as guilt is the aftermath of self-judging then we need to see the passive-aggressive nature of it. If anger was never OK with your family; if everyone had to be nice, and had to follow the rules; if there was never a space to ask why, or to question anything, then you had to keep the lid on your natural angry feelings. Passive aggression is the dysfunctioning of anger. When we can deal with our anger at our internal judge, we can begin the journey of healing guilt. Our internal judge sets goals for us, way beyond our capabilities, and not in a loving way of encouraging us to be all we can be, but laughs at us when we cannot reach them, and shames us into self-hate. The non-forgiving of ourselves is the ultimate act of self-hatred 'sin against the holy ghost – love' where I abandon myself to the hands of the inner tyrant produced by the earth-mind's conditioning. If I do not deal with guilt, depression sets in very quickly.

Exercise in Grace
dealing with guilt

Make a list of things in your life for which you feel guilty. Then write down what the voices of condemnation are saying to you. Then see the judge for what he is, and dialogue with him. Talk to all his voices. Get angry; get annoyed. Out the rage if there is any. Then write a letter to the judge. Tell him you did the best you could, and you are willing to forgive yourself, even if he is not.

After a while you will realize that this internal judge is your conditioned earth-mind, which is full of fear, full of anguish, and has tried simply to keep you on the straight and narrow. This judge too must be called to the place of compassion within you if your guilt is to be healed fully.

Exercise in Grace
dealing with fear

Deal with your fear as if it was a person. How would you deal with someone who is in fear? Place 'fear' on a cushion on a chair opposite you. Now speak to it, and ask it what it needs. See it as immature, and as one who has tried to keep you safe. Let it know that it is not appropriate for you to listen to the voice of destruction, and ask fear to come into your heart. This is what fear has longed for, but did not know how to ask for it.

Now go to the chair, take the cushion in your arms, and hug it. Feel the love float through you until your fear, or your judgemental self is wrapped in the love of your soul, and you both rejoice. This may take some time but do persevere. Fear is simply your earth-mind needing attention from your soul.

Whilst it would seem that women more easily allow themselves to express feelings, many women find it difficult to express anger. We seem to identify grief with tears, but not with anger. Guilt arising from the death of a loved one is usually the harsh judgements of ourselves – 'I could have done', 'I should have done', 'I ought to have'. The critical parent within ourselves prevents us from truly grieving, and letting go; in other words, I am not worthy to grieve. I am guilty. When I visited a concentration camp in Germany with a German friend, she said through her tears 'How could we grieve when we felt so guilty?' This reminded me of the collective guilt held in the psyche of German people.

One of the consequences of this type of collective guilt is a need for overachieving, reaching for perfection in everything. We must be seen by the rest of the world as being good if not perfect at something. This 'being seen to be perfect' is an attempt to cancel out the debt of guilt, internalized grief, and the perceived blame from others. Suppressed anger, leading to depression is also the outcome of such situations. According to Hitler, only those who could direct universal hatred to themselves could be saved. What a strange, dangerous so-called social manifesto to hand on to his people. What a legacy for German children to the fourth generation. One of the reasons I have a deep affiliation with German people, apart from our Celtic natures, is our collective sense of guilt. I, being an Irish woman, having lived in Northern Ireland for 24 years carry the crosses of a warring, raging people. I realized this when I started sharing with my German friends. 'Can anything good come out of Northern Ireland?' an English person asked me once. Unconsciously, I was going to prove that 'yes' something good can come out of Northern Ireland. I was going to be the best peace person around, and all the time I carried this unconscious sense of guilt at what 'my people' had perpetrated on their own, for the love of God and country. How easy it is for the victim to turn perpetrator.

My work in Germany since 1994 has enriched me and I am in awe at the determination of the people to heal the sins of the fathers. May I now, from a more conscious place, let the peace in my own heart flow outward, and help to heal the rifts and family splits in my own country. Peace begins in me.

> *Oh my country,*
> *Come and lay your history down.*
> *You have carried it far too long now.*
> *Come and lay your history down.*
> — *P. Anam-Áire*[vi]

Helpful guidelines for dealing
with guilt after the death of a loved one

Write a letter to the deceased, telling them all you really feel. Read it every day until you are no longer reacting to the contents, until you can read it with a sense of compassion, and love for you both. Dialogue with an empty chair, or with a photograph of the deceased. Talk to them as if they were really present. Share with him or her feelings of guilt, anger etc. Shout if needs be. Dialogue with your own internal critic, the voice that pronounces you guilty. Allow yourself to use any language you choose.

Call in your own wise, loving self, the part of you that is all compassion and love. Listen to the ways this wise person validates you. Hear that voice tell you 'Be gentle on yourself. Go in peace. Be guilty no more.' Write a long letter to yourself from that all-loving, understanding self. Read this letter everyday until you actually hear it in your heart, and feel it to be true. Hold a soft cushion to your heart. Let your tears of grief flow, tears for your beloved, and for yourself.

Guilt will eventually disappear, and self-esteem and self-compassion will take its place. You will no longer live in remorse (to die again), and will reach out in love and acceptance of life again. Guilt robs us of joy, for it is self-abandonment. Self-compassion helps us to lift up our hearts to integrate the harsh voices of the earth-mind, and eventually, let go of the critical parent who seeks only to control, and keep us safe. Eventually (and do not rush this stage) you will realize through your own experience that love never dies, life does not die, we are not going anywhere, all is transformation.

This realization comes only when you have given time for grief and time for healing. As long as we blame ourselves for the death of the other, we prevent the healing of active grieving. When people are helped to express their anger and that is simply stating what is not OK for them, saying no with inner authority, they realize that under their anger were tears of loss. It would seem that socially it is more acceptable for men to be angry, and for women to cry. After all, we educate young men to kill other men, never to grieve the ones they did kill or to meet with their relations, therefore, self-forgiveness and being forgiven is impossible. In Northern Ireland, I realized that men shoot other men because they had held in rage, which hardened their hearts. (They also held the rage of centuries, the rage of their ancestors.)

They needed a victim. I truly say that only a body, without life force/soul can take a gun and shoot another man, his neighbour. He has to be in an altered state of consciousness to do such acts of violence. A person who is truly conscious, and deals with their own dark shadow, cannot, and will not commit such atrocities. When we are in fear, any cause becomes a righteous reason to victimize another when we need to project our pain out there. May we all deal with the unfinished grief from childhood and contribute to real peace in our world. Peace begins in, and through me. *Seá*

The place of victim

When a child is disappointed at the parent's lack of physical contact, i.e., loving touch, expressions of love, verbal and symbolic, or their lack of empathy and understanding, the child withdraws and becomes depressed, or rebels and cries louder, sometimes without even knowing why. Depression and melancholy can set in at a very young age. This depression goes very deep into the unconscious and she becomes a victim. From this place of victim, she feels incapable of moving forward. The world becomes an unsafe place to live in as no one really cares, so the child withdraws from the outside world (often such a child enters a convent or becomes a monk in a silent community later on). The world of silence becomes her refuge as no one can hurt her there.

From this place of victim, a young child often takes on the role of caretaker, in order to get the love she needs. I adopted such a role at a very early age. I took care of my parent's needs, and demanded nothing for myself. I had my mother's smile at least, which was enough to make me happy. The more she smiled at me, the more I adapted to her need for peace and quiet in the home. I did likewise with my father. At an early age, I was able to tune into his moods, and adapt to them. If he was in a sad mood, I was very quiet, and neither seen nor heard. I was then a 'good, wee girl'. However, years later, I noticed myself adapting to a male co-worker in the same way. If he were in a good mood, I would sing and joke. If he were in a depressed mood, (like my father), I kept quiet. He never demanded this, of course, but old patterns die hard.

Self-absorption

Children react in many different ways, when their needs for love, and intimacy are denied, for example, many children become self-absorbed. They learned that people cannot, and often, do not, offer any solace. Sometimes indeed, a pet cat or dog, or even gerbil becomes the child's saviour, because the animal gives the love and warmth that a parent cannot give. If the child is allowed to rebel they will not carry the depression and melancholy, but will be able to go forward, with self-confidence. This, of course, leads to self-love, which is the antithesis of self-absorption or selfishness. The child's own internal authority grows, with a clear knowing of what she needs, and with the help of loving adults, she realizes that whilst the needs may not be necessarily met, there and then, that at least she has a right to ask for them, without being made wrong.

If however, the rebellious nature is seen as bad, or sinful, or bold, the child withdraws further, and anger is then directed at the self. Often, such a child will hurt herself in order to cope with the pain, or will recourse to bullying other children, and, as already referred to will hurt small animals. It is as though they need a victim on which to vent their pain. These children are not helped by our revenge and alienation; rather, they need our understanding and love. To provide a safe place for such children to vent their tears and rage is very necessary or their self-absorption continues into adult life, and the adult spends her day in self-pity, and self-centredness. (I have used large bean bags where children can vent their rage and scream their fears. Afterwards their creative juices flow).

Depressed, withdrawn children allow little things to get them down, and they react to every little inconvenience. They always put the blame out there, and find no comfort in their lives. When they form partnerships later on, childhood patterns are restimulated. That is why being in a relationship can be the healing of childhood dysfunctional patterns if we acknowledge them, and work towards releasing them.

Many adults are afraid of confrontation. The moment their partner behaves in what they deem to be 'unacceptable behaviour', saying no, they withdraw their love, and will not interact until the other behaves themselves, or stops 'being childish'. Blaming or criticizing the other for saying 'no' is also a reaction from childhood. Being angry was seen as bad and ugly, and so the old tape gets played in this relationship, which is no longer one of equality and respect. Stating their needs with inner authority brings out the critical parent in the other. These people make statements like 'When you behave like that I have no other choice but to withdraw from you.' and these reactions are straight from childhood, and from a place of victim. 'I have no other choice', clearly states I am helpless.

It was what was done to them. When an adult blames the other for her lack of joy and happiness, they are clearly operating from the past. Inner authority simply states needs, and this is not done in a loud or aggressive way. When your 'no' is not heard, consciously withdraw from the situation, not in anger or in helplessness and clearly state your needs at another time. This consciousness keeps you in your adult present.

Exercise in self-care

Start with today and decide what it is you wish for this day. You may not seem to have a choice in how you live it, and women in particular seem to have a need to juggle a few things all at the same time. It is a habit and it is also a way of controlling everything. But look again.

What would you like to change — transform? Is there a way whereby you can change some of the details of your day, so that you have time for doing something you really like and want to do? So you have to get the children to school, go to the supermarket, visit the doctor, visit a friend in hospital, and be home in time to make dinner for the family…wow!

Let us see how you can work this so you make time available for yourself. Can you allocate someone to take the children to school or go to the supermarket? When you come home from the doctors, is there a possibil-

ity you can sit down for half an hour and listen to your favourite music before you begin dinner? Is there a possibility that you do not have to do or be seen to be doing everything? The reallocation of your time during the day and allowing others to help in some way can truly give you time for yourself and your heart's wishes. But you need to call in your willpower in order to succeed in this.

You may have to let go of the control button and allow a friend or relative or your partner to help. Remember, if you seem to be coping with everything, you can even fool yourself into believing it is all working wonderfully. Then for some reason or other one day, you get annoyed at some trivial thing and the explosion happens. 'I never get help in this house; I have to do it all on my own. Wouldn't you think someone would see that I need help?' It is essential that you take time for the things you love to do, otherwise you will be resentful of the people around you.

Chapter 4

Exercises in Grace

Exercise 1
Expressing feelings

What does your life say to you this moment? What are your needs?
Do you feel loved, good enough, valued? Do you tell others and/or
children you love them, they are good enough, you value them?

The grateful heart receives twice

Do not wait until you meet a significant 'other' person, – a lover, a soul
mate – and then tell them how very important they are to you. Tell your
neighbour how grateful you are that they are close to you. Smile at people you don't know. Do not let an opportunity pass without
reminding/rehearting someone how good you feel that they are in your
life. If you find someone attractive, tell them. It does not mean you have
to start a deep relationship. Just tell them from your heart what you feel.
That is all. Then you can walk away having reminded/rehearted another
soul of their worth, their divinity. Who knows, by just doing that you
may have rekindled the flame of self-love in that person. Talk also to the
trees of their beauty, strength etc., also the flowers, children, anything or
anyone that creates a feeling of wellbeingness. If someone opens your
heart or touches you, tell them. Do not hold back your joy. When you
do, you hold back grace. Joy wipes out worry.

The earth-mind loves problems, and feels so important when it has a
problem to solve. It believes that its job is to solve problems! This makes
it feel superior: I am a solver of life! It tries to see life as a problem that
must be solved. When there is no problem, it creates one. Why don't I

have a problem to solve? Am I in denial, after all life is all about suffering, and problems are all about suffering? Look at your life; is it full of stress? Are you caught up in the attitude that you are here to suffer? Then you are not in the present moment, not in soul time, not in chronological time but caught up in the past/future continuum. Rigid goal setting and stressing about time limits to attain them promotes fear and anxiety.

Too much emphasis on positive thinking is release/escape from now, from acceptance of now. For example if I am annoyed with someone, or an event, I can either accept it or let it go or if you choose, let the other know so that you may release it. Alternatively, I can say I am not annoyed, I am at peace, and I am calm. Annoyance is a feeling/emotion that shows me I need to change a situation, and be responsible for my feelings. It is only a feeling, and feelings can change once we recognize them, feel them, accept them, let them go, with no attachment, and no resistance to them. But to deny the feeling, and pretend it does not exist is to live lies. The earth-mind solves the annoyance by lying, by pretending it does not exist. Similarly, the earth-mind solves the problem of illness by demanding that I lie and say I am well when I am not feeling well, or I am at peace when I do not feel at peace. Earth-mind wants to change me; the soul accepts where, and who I am, and allows change to happen by non-resistance to what is.

Write down the answers to the following questions without judging any of them:

— What feelings do you have difficulty expressing?
— Are you able to share your grief and tears?
— What do you do with your angry feelings?
— If someone hurts or annoys you, how do you deal with this?
— Do you still have temper tantrums?
— Are you able to state clearly your discontent with someone without having to 'go to war' with them?
— Do you sometimes/ever become passive aggressive, and shame or reduce another to the status of 'bold child'?
— If you are envious of a friend, what do you do about it? Remember sarcasm and cynicism is also about jealousy as it is about anger. Would you ever think of sharing this with them?

- Are you ever ashamed of your sexual fantasies?
- What do you mean by sexuality?
- Do you easily share your joy and good news with others?

We sometimes forget that the unconscious also holds the so-called light shadows like joy, fun, mercy, free child, dance, wildness, music. We need to be able to feel all this in our bones and express it, too, so that the joy in us, the ecstasy in us can find expression. When you are feeling happy, and joy fills your bones, do you ever share this with another? For me there is a great difference between 'happy' and 'joy'. To be happy necessitates an outer stimulus, something I can be happy about. Joy is in-dwelling love, the feeling that is beyond feeling because it does not necessitate outer stimuli. In my darkest moments I can still touch the hem of this great in-dweller. It is about our innate divinity that nothing and no one can destroy and is often hidden under our emotional unfinished business. This joy I wish my friends can connect with daily. This is the joy that I send out to all sentient beings because it does not come from my personality, but it is the divine in me touching the divine in the other, and this is real relationship. When we meet in this way we feel empowered, loved, and feel our own sense of worship.

We need to own our 'own goodness' and then we are capable of great things like calling back our projections, and forgiving our so-called enemies, helping those less fortunate than ourselves, enduring great pain with a sense of acceptance, smiling when it takes courage to do so, etc. Our light shadow and our dark shadow are the two sides of the coin of grace. Why not own our own goodness?

Exercise 2
Owning our golden shadow

Take time now to write down your 'good' attributes,
for instance:
Your own divinity
Your talents
Your joy at the good luck of another

The way you are there for your friends
The selfless way you visit people in hospital, etc.
Your honesty, trustworthiness, faithfulness
Your integrity

When you have the list written (and don't stop until you have at least twenty 'good' things to say for yourself!), ask a friend to witness it all for you. This will be difficult for many as we are so caught up with the idea of pride and self-centeredness. Humility is about knowing who we are, and living from that reality. It is not about denying our goodness.

Imagine if the first day you went to school the teacher said:

How great to see you, I look forward to learning so much from you. Let me know how you feel about being here. Thank you for coming here. I am honoured you chose our school. Think of the difference that might have made to your whole education! Imagine being praised for what you already knew before you came to school! Most of us were chastized for what we did not know, without any reference to what we did know.

A young man of farming background told me once: 'I knew far too much of what was not important and not enough of what was.' When I asked him what he meant by this, he answered: 'I knew how to rake the grass and feed the hens. I knew how calves are born. I knew when you milk the cow you must give her hay. I knew when it was midday as the flowers opened up then. I knew about rainbows after rain and thunder comes before lightening. I knew how to make the butter when the churning was done. I knew that dying was not dangerous. We lay in bed with our mother as she was dying and we hugged her goodbye. I knew it was important to help the neighbours take in the hay. You see I knew a lot but the teacher did not call that knowledge. Knowledge was being able to spell "Wednesday" and adding 16 and 13 and getting it right. Somehow I never saw myself as being any good.'

He went on to tell me how he was made to stand in a corner with a towel around his head whilst the other children chanted: 'Silly, silly Johnny can't spell Wednesday.' He was seven years old then. This young man's self-esteem was very low as it was difficult for him to accept that he could know anything that was not as he called it 'book learning'. So many of us find it difficult to own our sense of being alright; never mind calling ourselves holy.

Light being/dark being

In Hinduism, especially, we have the paradoxical deity of good and evil in the forms of *Shiva* and *Kali*. *Kali* the wife of *Shiva* was the feminine aspect that portrayed the dark destroyer of all. Indeed she was the great transformer, who like *Shiva* held compassion in her heart whilst at the same time wielded her sword of destruction.

In Celtic Consciousness, it seems that many of the gods and goddesses reigned over the worlds of darkness and light, the worlds of birth and death, the worlds of seeming duality, the worlds of paradox. It was as if one of the great attributes of a god or goddess was that they made no great distinction between dark and light, birth and death. *Bili* was the god of death or the dark, but his offspring were known as 'the children of light'. The god, *Lugh*, who was known as a sun god, was also lord of the underworld. The great god, *Dannan*, gave his lordship over the dark, or *an duach*, which was called 'the underworld' and also called 'the land of the living'.

We had to learn to fear the dark. The dark is also known in Christianity as the place where Lucifer, the 'prince of darkness' or the 'fallen angel' ruled; whilst the light was depicted as the 'bright angel' or the 'messenger of God's love', and we were advised strongly at school to cast from us all that is not light and bright and beautiful. (God himself sent the prince of darkness out of heaven as he could not bear to have a shadow!) This has been the doctrine of the patriarchy and has prevailed for centuries. It is not easy to step into a new gospel, one that accepts ourselves as 'children of the light', which is to include the dark. Like all gods, the archetype Brigit reigns in the underworld kingdoms of the unconscious and she maintained that all warring came from sending our fear and darkness into the world.

This fear and darkness eventually manifests as an entity in itself, and we cannot live the abundance of a rich and beauty-filled life whilst out there something fierce and dangerous is lurking. Our own fears and undealt-with emotions like revenge and envy become the boogey men, the enemies which we create, and which come back to haunt us. I believe that all our boogey men need to be loved back into our own psyche, where they can be transformed by love into grace. We have not been taught to do this and we have suffered consequently.

Dealing with the Judas within – our unfinished business

Judas' guilt and shame condemned him. His own sense of helplessness and despair condemned him. His self-hatred condemned him. His pain was so intolerable, that he could not stay with himself. The big lesson for us here is that each of us is Judas. The moment we sell ourselves – when we betray ourselves, when we dim our lights so that we do not speak our truth – we betray our souls. When we cannot say 'I am sorry', when we give ourselves away, and see ourselves as unworthy of love, or when we abuse ourselves by burning ourselves out or expecting way too much from ourselves, then in that moment, we take on the Judas archetype. We truly believe we are the unforgivable, the unlovable, and the untouchable. Our lack of self-compassion and our self-abandonment become the rope with which we hang ourselves. This in Celtic Consciousness is known as *ag cur an marbh orainn*, literally 'pronouncing our death sentence'. Self-compassion shows mercy to the internal Judas, and he does not have to suffer at our own hands.

If the Christ archetype is within us, the Judas archetype is within also; and this is difficult for many to accept. The way to holiness is to immediately forgive ourselves, so that we do not have to suffer from guilt and shame, which does not serve anyone. The Christ archetype within us has great compassion for the Judas. The lesson is to follow the voice of the beloved, or soul so that Judas can be loved back to where he belongs, sitting with the Christ. To exclude Judas, and see him as unworthy of our mercy, is to put Judas out into the world, and see him in others.

> *THE POINTED FINGER*
> *Let the finger pointed towards a friend*
> *Return in deep compassion towards thine self*
> *Lest in pointing shouldst thou stricken be*
> *In death's untimely hour*
> *Gods' judgement cast a spell on thee*
> *Under whose finger thou must surely cower.*
> C. McGill, (my grandfather 1930)

Exercise 3
Integrating the dark shadow

Think of a person you called arrogant?
What was it about them that was arrogant?

OK, now remember a time in your life when you were arrogant.
Go back as far as you need to, and invite that part of you into your
consciousness.
Good! You have found that lost part of yourself. Well done!

Now ask that part of you to come into your heart.
What does it feel like?

Allow yourelf to realize that you are not a bad person because you have
been arrogant. It was the only way you could have behaved at the time
with the limited knowledge you had.

Now forgive yourself.

Now see the part as being accepted by the so-called 'good' part of you. –
See them embrace. Great! You have called that lost part of you home.

The time will come when you will be able to go to the other person and talk to them about it. You have forgiven yourself so you can ask for forgiveness. If the other is still annoyed, that is their way, do not get caught up in their business.

Now you are getting to know what Brigit means by holiness!

The so-called stay-at-home 'good parts', our light shadows, need to be honoured by us, we need to know our own angel-self, our own divinity, so that when the dark shadows seek refuge we do not discard them but fully integrate them in mercy.

A timing for all things

This teaching is important because it does not advocate rushing to change what is not acceptable in our lives. It would suggest that everything has its own rhythm, and to interrupt it or try to manipulate it is unwise. Awareness is the key word here. Being aware of our need for change allows change to happen. Nature is our role model. She will not rush the seasons just because she wants change. We are also advised that women's rhythms are not like those of the male. She needs at least 28 days to integrate her intuitive knowing with her intellectual assessment if asked to initiate a major change in her life. Women's deep intuition signals to her when change is necessary. If she ignores such promptings, she answers from her earth-mind only and so, may feel confused later on.

Exercise 4
Intuition

— *Do you often get 'gut feelings' about a person or things but ignore them; only to find out later you would have been wiser to follow them? Learn to listen inwardly; it is the way of integrity and grace, and the way of the Creator. When you listen internally first, what you bring out will be a blessing.*

The soul also loves simplicity, and loves that moment of 'aha'. The way of intuition is the opposite of illusion; it is the place where dualism is loved home. Our heart feels the impulses of intuition, and when we listen with our hearts we listen to the soul. The wise heart carries with it the gifts of discernment and integrity. The immature heart carries with it the wants of our earth-minds. Learning to differentiate between the two hearts comes from being able to recognize our inner voices. Our intuition is soul imbued, our earth-minds are wants imbued. When we listen with that inner wisdom we tune into the knowing of our ancestors who sensed the world from the inside out.

Intuition is more than just instinct. It is instinct with consciousness and creativity. It is that place where the earth-mind's conditioning gives way to the soul's all knowing. Intuition does not need to analyze, to conceptualize, to have sound reasons, to have good calculations, or even to have logic. In actual fact, intuition is the antithesis of these. Let us learn to create within us the mind of the Christ, the mind of Buddha, the mind of the child, uncluttered yet marvellous in its simplicity, and full of awe. Intuition 'understands', and knows about paradox. Indeed, paradox is the essence of intuition. As Hannah Cunningham points out, 'To intuit is to *know*, to intellectualize is to *theorize*.'

Intuitive choice is not something that one can project into the future. It is immediate, for now, for this moment and does not necessarily mean that the decision we make from our intuition today is right for all time. This can be confusing for many who want the decision to be right forever and ever. When I met my last partner I thought he was right for me. I thought the relationship was forever! After four years I realized that the intuitive thought was right for then – that he was right *for that time* – and I was not wrong to take the leap of faith *at that time*. The gifts of self-knowing I received from the connection were like precious jewels. The only problem was that I wanted it to last and that was not the nature of the relationship.

Chapter 5

Goddess Archetypes

The triple goddess
– triple archetypes

Brigit 'in-bodies' the archetypes of triple goddess in the integration of Virgin, Mother, and Crone. These rich attributes imbue her with all the manifestations of the divine or holy feminine to include the antithesis of all. What does the attribute of Virgin have to offer us today? We will look at it firstly with reference to the young woman, pre-Motherhood, and then we will consider the counterpart in the male genre.

The triple goddess

The triple goddess is symbolized by the colours white, red, and black.

White symbolizes Virgin, or she who truly knows herself. In the male counterpart it is Youth, or uninitiate – still in the house of the Mother; he who has not yet received the Father's going-out blessing.

Red symbolizes mothering, or the red blood of passion and creativity. For the male it symbolizes the red of passionate sexuality, the energy of the sunset and the questing for his Father's fathers.

Black symbolizes the Wise Woman, and her ability to transform herself. She chooses wisely and with integrity. She is the one who has inner authority, and is allowed to give the Woman's blessing. In the Male it symbolizes the one who has integrated his anima and animus, and is allowed to advise the younger men about life, and women! He tells the stories about his Father, and has little or no regrets.

The Virgin *(an Maighdean)*

It would seem that the usual meaning of the word, 'a maiden who has never been penetrated sexually by a male' does not fit here. It is too rigid. The word 'virgin' in the old Gaelic meant 'one who calls herself to life', in other words a young woman who has not yet mothered, but who gets to know her own self. She is someone who is willing to birth her soul to her body. The idea of Virgin is also about the naivety or innocence with which we come to birth – innocence of intention, innocence of motivation. The young woman is usually motivated only by her heart's desires. She feels her world as opposed to rationalizing it. Expressing feelings is natural to Virgin. Her sense of individuation happens at puberty as she enters into the stirrings in her lower body through menstruation. The lower chakras, or energy centres, are the natural human building blocks of a strong and effective earth-mind, without which we could not survive in our world.

That virginal state of sturdy trust holding out against the whirlwinds of betrayal and change is often seen in young girls as they experience the breaking of their hearts in love. They break the heart open, get up, brush themselves down, and go for it again. This 'undaunted by negative experience'self is the energy of Virgin. It is also the place of ordinary magick, where Youthfulness and daring show off their prowess to an overcautious world which shakes its weary head in disapproval.

If however, the Mother of the Virgin manipulates her boldness and challenges her to be less proud and more demure; she will end up in a place of self-hatred, and will diminish in stature. If the Mother has not integrated her own Virginity, she will no doubt, through jealousy and dominance, kill off the innocence in her daughter, who will be left full of guilt and shame. The story of Cinderella and her cruel stepmother shows the intense envy of the dysfunctioning step-in-Mother for her daughter. Cinderella's beauty and youthfulness infuriated her. She could not delight in her because she had not surrendered to her own aging process with grace, therefore, imposed suffering on her young daughter to alleviate her own pain of envy.

Virgin is not one to postpone anything in her life. She believes in living in the moment. If she is sad, she expresses it. Likewise if she feels angry, she lets the steam rise and in a moment it is over and she is happily engaged in something else. She trusts her feelings, and is not ashamed to show them. We know that young Persephone will soon be taken to the underworld, by an unsuspecting lover and we older women long for her return in us, for she is a re-hearter (reminder) of our own beauty, albeit now internalized. We have lost much of our exuberance for and in life because we have tamed the Virgin in us, and have replaced her with a rigid set of rules that restrict her creativity and emotional growth. Sadly, we forget the times when we also allowed ourselves to take risks, and live fully in the present moment with no fear of tomorrow. It is however the unintegrated Virgin in us that burns herself out, that does not know when to limit her resources.

Exercise 1
Risk taking

Virgin asks you if you really know who you are. She asks you to live your life fully before you die. Should you hear her whisper in your ears 'Go for it, realize your dreams.' then do so, and spend that extra money, and join a dance group, and forget the neighbours! What are the dreams you allowed to die in you as opposed to letting go of unattainable dreams?

— *Do you procrastinate?*
— *Listen to the words of this song and then write down what they mean to you today.*

> ### No Blame
> *Are you living the life that you want to?*
> *Are you living out somebody's dream?*
> *Do you love the one that you sleep with?*
> *Is your life really not what it seems?*
> — *P. Anam-Áire*[vii]

Prayer to the Virgin in Us
Virgin, show me my innocence,
Open my heart to love,
Dance my life
To the flesh of my own drum.

The Youth *(an Óige)*

If Virgin is an archetype of the triple goddess, then Youth is the male counterpart, also within her psyche, for she is without genre or discrimination. Whilst the place of Youth is found in both young male and female persons, it is normally defined as 'a young man or boy'. Somehow it is not associated with sexuality as is Virgin. One might be inclined to imagine therefore that sexuality is a more important component of the young female psyche, and is therefore written into the name itself.

The Youth is that place of discovery and experience. Not to be mistaken for similar attributes of Virgin. Foolishness and Youth are synonymous it would seem. It suggests acting from a place of 'natural' as opposed to 'normal' ie conditioned. It is about being free to choose. This foolishness is mostly about 'misspent Youth'. In other words it suggests a time of exploration, adventure, and distraction for the sake of excitement and fun. The Youth archetype of goddess refers to the place of non-responsibility and wildness. That is not to say it is dangerous territory, and therefore needs to be captured and controlled. On the contrary it is a living organism of vital and life-giving juices, deriving its impetus from nature herself.

The dynamism of the Youth when shown his own particular magick and wonder can enliven him with creativity beyond his wildest dreams. Youth needs a Father, who has not lost his own Youthfulness within to support him. If the Father is patriarchal, and uses abusive tactics to tame the young man's wilderness characteristics, then the soul of the Youth will wither and die. When Youth is allowed full expression of who he is, with the understanding energy of Father supporting him, his creative impulses flow and his animal self can be free to dance his wild dance of sheer life-force energy upon the earth. It is said that when Youth dances the animal in him alive with no sense of shame, or embarrassment, the earth chants back a song, and the ancestors join in.

Exercise 2
Suppressing the natural wilderness

— *When did Youth in you perish?*
— *When did you last pull your knapsack onto your shoulders, and for the sheer fun of it without any end-gaining plans, or well mapped-out routes, take yourself off for a weekend of adventure?*
— *When did you last distract yourself from the mundane adult responsibilities by eg., singing in a band, or hugging a tree?*

The saddest words I have ever heard from someone dying were 'I wish I had done what my heart wanted to do instead of always doing the *right* thing.' Remember: all work and no play make Jack a dull boy.

— *Do you have others who share your enthusiasm for life?*
— *Have you lost interest in the world around you because no one will give you what you need?*
— *Remember the Youth in you says: 'Life is precious, it is yours to make what you will of it; you are the author of your days.'*
— *Do you live in the past as if that is all there is to your life?*

There is still time for the Youth to have his say in you even if you are 70 years old, but you need to listen and be willing to take risks!

> *PRAYER TO THE YOUTH IN US*
> *Youth of my wilderness ways,*
> *Pour your swift feet*
> *Into my tired legs*
> *And hurl me beyond my own borders.*
> *Seá*

The Mother *(an Mathair)*

The term 'mother' naturally suggests passion, sexuality, birthing, nurturing, giving, and caring. It is said of Brigit that 'the red blood from her body nurtures all creation' and the red berries of the ivy tree are but drops of her blood. The bleeding woman knows about death, and life; she dies every 28 days and resurrects herself. It was also said by our ancestors that her menstrual blood holds mystery and magick. This was one of the reasons why woman went apart from the group gatherings for three days when she was bleeding, so that she could become more consciously aware of her psychic powers and create healing potions.

The Mother archetype is very powerful. It holds within it the very miracle of life itself. She is co-creator, and as such she has fierce and wondrous power, and her knowing is intuitive. She is mighty in her protective impulses regarding her offspring, and would kill if necessary any predator lurking in the shadows. Mother is a place of deep commitment to a cause or person. It is the place of responsibility and dependability. The red colour not only suggests the significance of the blood issue, but also it is indicative of the full red passionate woman who may not decide to procreate.

Mother may use her blood passion in various different ways for the good of all. Many women still bleeding create wonderful spaces for others to explore their own lives; she may be a teacher of children, a nurse in a hospital, a counselor, or a poet. Or she may decide to use her passionate nature in her exploration of her sexual nature, by keeping it alive, and using orgasm to infuse her with deeper psychic powers. This, many *Seabhéans* (Wise Women) do in the Celtic tradition.

The feeding Mother has been depicted in art and sculpture as the nurturer of the young, the one who feeds another from her own body. Woman's breasts have been used in the commercial world to persuade the populace to purchase goods from cars to bars of soap. Such is their attraction. Their initial purpose – to feed babies – has been so manipulated by the media that some women refuse to breast feed because of fear of 'drooping breasts syndrome'. However, many women are continuing the natural method of nurturing their young despite the caution of flagging breasts. They see that the great privilege of feeding their young is an act of deep, deep, love and devotion, and one that will bring its own healing results. The example of the powerful sexual energy of woman is depicted by *Sheela-na-gig*, the Irish goddess of fertility. Her overt sexuality is shown by her squatting posture with her hands opening her vagina like an enchanted cave for all to behold and enter. Her sexuality was symbolic of the open graciousness of the great Mother Earth, and her fertile and rich harvesting.

When Patrick came to Ireland in the fifth century, his Youthfulness could not cope with womanpower so he symbolically drove her out by casting the snake from the island. The images of Sheila-na-gig were erased from most churches and monasteries and were replaced with icons of the Virgin Mary with her cloak of blue. Art works, such as Michelangelo's Madonna, were tolerated later because of their artistic contents, and were not so sexually explicit. The fathers of the church however demanded that woman cover up, and shut up. They silenced her knowing and denied her healing powers.

Most Eastern religions embraced sexuality as a form of worship, and tantric sex has liberated many into the fullness and richness of relationship, and has deemed sex to be holy. Sexuality is now, more and more, being viewed within our Western culture as an expression of the sacred, and thanks to the work of more radical teachers we are beginning to accept a gospel of holiness that included the body in worship. Eros is being liberated and we rejoice.

The bleeding woman's natural psychic powers and healing qualities, whilst no longer hushed at the stake of patriarchy or relegated to a psychiatric hospital ward 'for further investigation', are still subdued. Women today can and do perform rituals of great initiation and transformation whilst bleeding. May our daughters be blessed by our willingness to bring back the blessings.

Exercise 3
Self-nurture

— How might the Mother archetype challenge you today?
— What are you passionate about?
— How do you feed your soul?
— Do you care for others out of duty?

- *When did you last decide to initiate sexuality in your relationship as part of your spiritual practice?*
- *How do you feel about your own body? Do you compare it to others younger or older than yourself?*
- *Do you judge yourself as having been a bad parent? What are the judgements you make of yourself?*

Take time to write down the answers to these questions. There is no right or wrong answer. This is an exercise for you to engage with your own feelings about how you see yourself.

These and other questions are from grace. Your honest reply will be indicative of how you have invited soul into your life. If you see yourself as an OK person without reproach, then you are listening to your soul song in you. If not, apart from immoral, and deliberately abusive actions, can you accept that you did the best you could, seeing the struggle you had in your own life at that time?

When you can look on your life with the mercy and honouring of the Mother, you will have begun the journey of self-healing. When you can allow yourself time to be creative, to attend that pottery class or whatever, you will be listening to the Mother in you, and she will bless you.

> **PRAYER TO THE MOTHER IN US**
> *Mother, of the deepest mercy,*
> *May I see me through your eyes.*
> *Gather me home*
> *When my own judgements*
> *Break my heart.*

The Father *(An Athair)*

Father archetype is seen as cohort and mate to Mother. Her knowing is from intuition whilst his comes from his involvement with the outer. He senses from the environment, and she from her womb. Father energy within the soul is expressed in his instinctual involvement with the elements. The outer reflects soul's inner landscape, in so far as she can project onto it her reality. Soul's swift all seeingness as perceived through the eyes of Father says: 'Don't mess with me.' She does not have to roar her disapproval; soul's inner authority reflects it in his eyes.

When Father (animus) archetype visits you, you will feel that inner authority, that sense of protection and strength that can carry you through the deepest pain. This is the voice of encouragement and praise, the voice of the truest honouring of your soul's wilderness. You can express your dance knowing he is holding a space for you to dance in. When you disregard his voice of caution you will become ill. People who express their soul energy in an artistic and extrovert way need the containing protection of Father in order to stay centred amidst their passionate involvement with life. Many artistic people resort to substance dependency, and often take themselves to the edge with their creativity with no boundaries to protect them.

This leads to further types of dependency, if they do not listen to the wisdom in the guiding voice of the internal functioning Father. The dysfunctioning Father seems to have been our guide for most of our lives. It is difficult therefore to feel the voice of approval amidst such disapproval. Jesus the Christ received a blessing from his Father. How many men, young and old, are longing for the Father to bless them, and so launch them forward into the world, secure in the knowing that 'all is well, I have the blessing of my Father'. Many women have excellent visions and dreams, but never seem to be able to activate them.

The Father archetype in them can help them realize their potential, help them ground their dreams in the here and now. Without this energy many women remain barren, unfulfilled, never actualizing their ideas. In truth the functioning or loving Father helps us to take risks that expand our awareness, and still create a home for us to lay our burdens down when we need to. He is the one who takes us beyond fear: fear of making a mistake, fear of losing, of being a failure. Whatever we do because of fear or don't do because of fear keeps us controlled by fear.

Exercise 4
I will, I won't

— *What don't you do 'just in case'?*
— *On the left side of a page write in big letters 'All the things I would love to do'.*
— *In the middle of the page write in big letters the words 'But I won't just in case'.*
— *Now, on the right side write down all the things you would passionately love to do.*

Go wild; be indulgent. You might be surprised to see the way fear rules your life.

Our fear of hurting others, of appearing silly in the eyes of our neighbours prevents us from having our will done. Mostly, people are afraid to make choices from the heart because they have been hurt before from having done so. They hide away 'for fear' or 'just in case' they might suffer again. This way fear takes over and the soul is unable to widen into the whole of the person.

> *Words from the song 'No Blame' give expression to this:*
> *Are you scared, if you change they won't like you?*
> *Are you scared, if you don't you will die?*
> *Are you living in fear of tomorrow?*
> *So you're living today with a lie?*
> — *P. Anam-Áire* [viii]

Do you feel safe to take risks for your soul's sake – for the sake of living fully your life here in earth? Do you ever feel you would like to rise above your fears and obsessions, but are afraid of becoming too vulnerable? For sure, you need the energy of the Father, the enabler, the guardian. He might give you 'tough love'; that is he might take you to the edge and show you you can fly, and assure you you can do it.

PRAYER TO THE FATHER IN US
Father in me, stay close to my Soul,
Guardian of my foolish ways,
Hold all my dreams
And give flesh to those
Held prisoner of fear…

The Crone *(An Cailleadh)*

The Crone archetype is the most complex of the three, for she holds within her the other two, namely Virgin and Mother. She represents the wise old woman having brought forth her children and who now grand-mothers all the children in the community. The Mother and Virgin parts visit her within her own psyche in times of pain and suffering. She patiently listens to all stories and then makes her appraisal from a place of balance. Crone is a place of acceptance, and a willingness to look at death and life straight in the face. She does not suffer fools gladly, but susses out through her wiles and inner knowing what lies beneath the surface of things. In the time of the Celts, each community or clan had its own Crone or Wise Woman to keep the old ways of the tribe alive and functioning.

I recall an old woman in our parish in Donegal whose name was Bid-dy who had answers for everyone whether they wanted them or not. With her smoky hair and black fingernails she smelt of fire burning, and her quick wit and intuition unsettled many. Biddy was able to 'see beyond the mountain on all sides' and was known to put spells on peo-ple who scorned her. She had little time for the clergy as she called them 'them men of the cloth and their lying stories about hell and damnation'.

Crone was known as the 'keeper of my-story/stories' or 'the one who takes care of the sacred or mysterious in each person'. In the Gaelic lan-guage she is known as the *Seabhean* or 'Wise Woman'. Women of her stature and calibre were known to have access to the underworlds. At the time of birthing and dying in the community she was called upon to administer the rituals, if the priestess was not available to perform them.

When she looks longingly out from her deep smoky eyes she sees more than the physical eyes. In the Gaelic language we say: *cionn an Seabhean ös ärd na greine*, meaning: 'the old one sees from the top of the sun'. The Croning ceremony, which I perform, celebrates the older woman in our midst. It honours the place of experience over theory. It honours the place of service from the soul rather than service from duty. Topics such as sexual abuse and death are often spoken of in hushed notes in our society. Crone talks openly and unashamedly about community issues, and is not afraid to openly discuss the sexual abuse of children, or unfaithfulness in marriage. Her role as elder allows her to teach especially about the stages of death and the *aites*, to which the person travels afterwards.

Birth is also her forte. In the far distant past Crone was present at births, taking care of the new birthed soul, making sure it was welcomed and blessed. Crone casts disapproval on anything that is not natural or honest. You cannot fool her for too long. She creeps up in your dreams if you ignore her. If you divert from your soul's chosen course, Crone will nudge you back on the road again. She sits and makes strange sounds in her throat, sounds like the crow and the raven. She is no stranger to the animal kingdom. She has understood the relationship between the anima in animals, and the anima in humans.

If Crone had her way, she would live in close proximity with the animals. Her belief is that we are not too far removed from them so she talks to them, and often prays to them for strength and centredness. She understands the seasons as they come and go as nature is her teacher in everything. She believes we have no right to own anything, either land or people. On the contrary her belief is that the earth owns us and she wisely teaches us the detachment in all things.

Crone is that place in woman that is older than her years, and younger than her dreams. That place where nature herself resides in the flesh and bones of our wild natures. Often a young maiden will display some of this wisdom. They are the truth sayers who at times embarrass their parents into honest and truthful communication. It is the Crone in us that laughs out loud at her own jokes! She makes no apology for loud laughter in the midst of seemingly serious debate because she is able to see the illusion of things and knows that all things are passing. What others might say of her no longer interests her as she has long ago let go of the opinion of others. At a deeper level of consciousness Crone invites us all, men and women alike, to become more conscious, to get in touch with our inner knowing that we had to suppress or exchange for academic achievement.

The older woman who has stopped bleeding was said to be in touch with the other worlds and have the ability to cross these worlds at ease. It was said that that was one of the reasons older women talk to themselves. They converse with other worlds within themselves. The Crone archetype in Brigit manifests in the way she becomes involved with issues of death and dying. She also shows herself in the building up of the hearth and keeping the fires lit. Brigit was known as the keeper of the hearth, the woman who could blow on the cold wood in the grate, and fire would leap from the hearth. She invites us all to burn in her flame, that which no longer serves us in our daily lives. What does not serve you, does not serve others. This statement seems radical, but then Brigit's teachings from the Cauldron are radical these days.

Exercise 5
Inner wisdom

— *Are you a 'people pleaser'?*
— *Do you ever go into nature and ask her guidance for your life?*
— *Are you able and willing to see the two sides to every story?*
— *How do you feel about death and dying?*
— *Are you able to see the funny side of life as well as the serious?*

Crone in you will help you to take things easy; to relax into the difficult spaces in your life and know that all is 'grist for the mill' of love's healing energy. She it is who whispers 'All is fine, do not worry my child.'

> **PRAYER TO THE CRONE IN US**
> *Knower of my secret thoughts,*
> *Speaker of wisdom in me,*
> *Older than the dark dark earth,*
> *Light your pipe in me.*

The Wise Man *(An Eolath)*

When some men get in touch with their 'Wise Man' around the age of 49, often their worlds fall apart. It is as if they can no longer rely on the old paradigms for clarity in decision-making. Rational thinking that excludes their own experience of life is no longer sufficient. It seems that they begin to operate from a very different perspective than just intellectual understanding. They have a need to turn back, to go a different route to the known one they had travelled so long. It is the *trasna*, the 'crossroads'. That place where transformation takes place within their psyche, and unless they begin to obey their soul song they feel they will perish. Men who suffer from burnout because of the driven dysfunctioning animus, out of which they have perceived their world for so long, begin to feel disappointed at the way they have chosen work over love or time with their children. They begin to realize what they are missing out on, and start to rearrange their lives accordingly. This is not easy as habits are difficult to change especially if they are the breadwinners, and still have mouths to feed.

Some men seek relationships outside their present one, and are attracted to younger, more adoring females. It is as if they fear the ageing process and can delay and deny it by attracting younger women. Men have been abused, and have been told lies by the patriarchy. They believe they have to be in control of everything or their worlds would fall apart. They have been used and abused in industry, commerce, and the armed forces as merchandise in the hands of political and economic structures. Their status in the workplace, which dictates their earning capacity, has been the evaluating criteria as opposed to virtues of soul such as kindness, mercy, loving fathering, good friend, upholder of feminine values and norms, etc.

The Wise Man in men challenges his sense of self-honouring and self-control. This entails coming to terms with the anima or soul-self. This soul-self is not interested in outer evaluation as his sense of who he is comes from a deeper knowing. And that deeper knowing is from the Wise Man. Brigit has been encouraging men to become more conscious in their choice making, to stop operating from a robotical model of existence and begin to live life from the heart. Many men suffer heart attacks, and complain of other heart-related illnesses. Maybe it has something to do with choices that need to be made with the heart in (the) mind. Men are now beginning to feel their emotions and express them appropriately. More and more men are gathering to share their lives, and contemporary Wise Men are encouraging men of all backgrounds to tell their stories, and heal their lives. They have heard the call of soul in their veins, their anima sings a love song to their stereotypical world values, and changes in the corporate world are happening daily.

Language is changing, and words like 'abundance' and 'mercy' are no longer confined to poets and singers. Men are no longer afraid of touching and hugging each other when they meet, although I smile when I see men still beating each other on the back as a form of greeting! It is as if no tenderness is seen to be allowed. But they are learning, and more and more men are demonstrating the functioning animus, and like the pied piper they entice other men out of their old conditioned roles to follow them; and many come. This is not about encouraging men to become effeminate, but to allow all of their male selves to shine.

In the past, men who have gone to war and killed 'the enemy' were called brave because they risked their lives for others. This was very commendable. Warriors of the heart however, do not fight battles out there, but with compassion for self and others courageously heal their lives. For me, bravery is about physical feats like air/sea rescue, fire fighting, policing difficult areas etc. It has to do with a personal contribution to society that goes beyond fear, and the primal 'flight or fight' instinct. They are acts of great mercy in the face of personal injury or death.

On the other hand courage for me is about personal heart opening. It is about subjective experiences, which though not seemingly risk taking or life threatening, entail the breaking open of the heart, and the willingness to go deeper and deeper into the world of pain for the sake of love. By this I mean the man who has had his heart broken in a long-term relationship, is willing to heal his own part in the break up, and then risk the further splitting of the heart open by daring to love again. This man I call courageous. When a man combines bravery with courage he lives compassionately, and with passion. He is indeed a Wise Man.

Exercise 6
What controls you?

– *When did you last speak to yourself with the patience of a good Father?*
– *When have you really listened to your own heart's longings without criticism?*
– *When did you last say no to an offer to work late at night because you wanted to see your children before they went to bed? Or because you needed that time for yourself to be with yourself and simply not do anything?*
– *When was the last time you gave an answer from your inner wisdom of experience rather from the textbook at the firm's general meeting?*
– *Have you decided to do some deep thinking about your affairs before you die?*
– *Does thinking of dying scare you?*
– *Are you afraid of letting go of your family, your status, your job, and your name?*
– *Who are you, without your job, your family, and your name?*
– *Are you driven to succeed or are you able to pace your work schedule to suit yourself?*
– *Are you taking good care of your health?*
– *Do you drink a little too much to help you relax after a hard day working?*

Today is a good day to share these thoughts. Why not write your answers on a piece of paper and invite your friends to do likewise. This is a good way to get in touch with the Wise Man energy in you. When I met with Walter Lechler MD in Bad Herrenalb, Germany, I immediately tuned into the Wise Man energy in him. He is the kind of man whose wisdom complimented my woman's knowing. We sat for ages sometimes just smiling at each other as language was not important. I am blessed to have such wise and beauty-full men in my life.

> **PRAYER TO THE WISE MAN IN US**
> *Oh! Wisdom of ages,*
> *Pour out your ancient knowing on my foolish bones,*
> *Light your fires of patience in my blood*

And tell the story of my days through your mouth.
Soul in our midst is the feeling self that urges us all to awaken to our
true nature, which is innate greatness. It is time to become independ-
ent of tribal philosophies that dictate our potential. It is time to
acknowledge that holiness or wholeness is about inclusiveness.
Move; move out to the edges of yourself,
Move out to where fear and love dance together
Move, move in, and embrace in love.
The Beloved resides at the edge of your small self.
Take her by the hand, and move, expand, stretch
Into life's abundance
– P. Anam-Áire 1998

Fear

Fear would tell you not to open your heart to the universe. If you do so you risk betrayal and ridicule. It says: 'Stay closed. Stay in your safe cocoon, inside your shell of what you think is protection.' Predators are waiting to devour you it advises. In your naivety, you obey for that is all you know up to now. In the darkness you cry out: 'I am alone. No one loves me. I am forgotten by everyone.' Sometimes you believe that love has also left you. Ah dear one, how well you have obeyed the voice of fear. How well you have attended to its advice. Life, on the other hand calls to you on so many levels but you cannot hear its voice, nor are you able to discern its presence.

Life says: 'Come take my hand, breathe into me, and breathe out into the universe. You are no longer the tiny child of yesterday. You are no longer the helpless victim of the past conditioning. You can express your feelings, heal the discordance, and dance a dance of joyful expansion.' I ask you this: do not hold yourself to ransom any longer than this breath. See now it is daybreak; the lonely night is over. The dark is not an enemy and life is not the enemy. Fear of life is the only restriction. Your time inside your imprisoned self was hell on earth. But it was the soul's precious time of experiencing alienation in order to emerge from it, and so comprehend the dark, and befriend it at last. The dark has no reality except the one you give it. Your addiction to the pain has given it reality where none was intended. It is as precious as the light. When you can realize this in your life, you will have broken the hold that fear has on you, and you will rejoice in the expansion of your chosen life on earth.

My friends, it was never your soul's intent to remain in the illusion of joylessness. But you insist on returning to the illusion as if it held all the wisdom. The illusory aspects of fear were there for the purpose of experiencing pain in order to emerge from it, and to have learned the particular lessons you needed to learn from its teaching. Imagine if you can come to each new moment with the innocence and enthusiasm of a child, of a Buddha, of a Christ.

Attributes of a holy person

— *Able to be fully in the body yet not overly identified with it.*
— *Lives in the now.*
— *Not surprised by change.*
— *Reviews life in a clear uncritical way.*
— *Able to forgive themselves.*
— *Accepts when they have made a mistake, and apologizes.*
— *Sees through the illusion of things and does not get caught up in the importance of unimportant things.*
— *Is used to joy, not surprised by ecstasy.*
— *Able to experience intense feelings without attachment.*
— *Deals with dysfunctioning feelings: revenge, envy, selfishness, hatred, etc. whilst in the body.*
— *Will challenge from a place of unattachment.*
— *Is at one with all creation.*

Chapter 6

The Cauldron of Wisdom

Universal soul *(Anam úilioch)*

Celtic Consciousness speaks of wisdom, which may also be named 'compassion'. As Brigit is synonymous with universal soul she is synonymous also with nature. She is unconditional love which earths the divine in us, that which longs for our healing through our humanness. For too long we have been immersed in the patriarchal definition of holiness, definitions of which have supported only the maleness of God, and have denounced the body, our earth, our clay, as a legitimate vehicle of grace and devotion. In a television programme some time ago, a Tibetan Buddhist nun sadly proclaimed that as a woman she cannot be enlightened this time. She had to pray to incarnate as a man next time. I cried when I heard these words. She exposed that Tara was the highest of Buddhist deities, the Great Mother who was ever ready to come to the aid of earth children. This seems to contradict what Buddhist women in general have been made to believe. Brigit like Tara had deep concern for suffering humanity, and they both show us that gender and cultural differences are not boundaries to enlightenment.

In the return of the Brigit archetype, emphasis on the genderless aspects of the creator helps reinstate us vagrants in the family of creation. Brigit does not confine her gifts and healing to just one culturally defined race of people. Her magick is in the spreading of her gifts all over the place, like the golden eagle; although like the eagle, we cannot hold her in material form. We feel, we sense, we touch, and we experience her essence through our own soul's longing to touch the gold in us. Words attributed to her are: 'I will come to my people when their clay is wet with the tears of their longing.' A male poet from 19th.century expresses his love of nature specifically because she was not male. To him nature symbolized freedom, contentment and inner stillness through her feminine face. He was able to recognize these gifts in nature as he saw the constraints, lack of hope and alienation within his own maleness. Nature for him was a retreat and balance.

Brigit is clear in her pleading with us to move from the constraints of confrontation to communication, politically and personally. Since the 60s some of us have been in training for the evolution of our souls. These lines which I attribute to Brigit can also be attributed to our individual souls, which are fragments from universal soul, and contain no less divinity.

> She is the fair one amongst us
> Heaven lightening from her eyes
> Sorrow cradled between her breasts
> The flying raven amongst her thighs.

Who indeed is this fair one, if not the very word made flesh in everyone of us, willing to go beyond our fear and say yes to our soul's song. She is the cradler of our sorrows and the dancer of our delights. She is the *challenger* in us human beings to live consciously with all creation. She is the *encourager* in us to be great, to stop looking up or out or over or back for our salvation, but to look within. She is the inner small or loud *voice* that beckons us back home into ourselves when we have wandered on another's route. She is the *strength* that supports us to go beyond fear, to go beyond the traditional tribal cautions and judgements of our ancestors and risk living fully our chosen lives in the earth. She is the *echo* of our own heartbeat that we sometimes strangle so as not to hear its pleadings with us to be wildly in love with our soul's energy.

She is the *soul* in each and all, singing a wilderness song to the domesticated parts of us, hoping we will stop and listen and burst open and break through. She is the great *anima*, the *experiencer* of the life of spirit in men and women, the *ancient call* to come into life fully and wondrously. She is the *paradoxical* madness that invites us to be at ease with chaos and confusion, and to see the alchemy of transformational grace in our eventual surrender of faith and hope. She is the *ripper* of our carefully sewn dreams. She does not offer happiness or niceties. She is the *offerer* of full participation in life here and now, and has no time to waste on our well-considered rationality.

She does not hand us a well thought-out map landmarking danger-ous territories to avoid, or scenic routes to rest in. She simply *encourages*: take the first step on the journey and just be willing to keep on walking. She ASKS us to keep our hearts open for everything and all. She *teaches* us the language of feelings. This is where most of us tremble at the knees. We are mostly not prepared to feel. We have been taught that feelings can be dangerous company. They lead us into all sorts of trouble and apart from the so-called good feelings like love and happiness, when we hear about expressing feelings we hear grief, anger and sadness. We somehow hear the dark side and we just close down out of fear.

Universal heart *(Croi úilioch)*

Only when the heart is broken open can compassion flow through. But does the heart actually break? Why do we use this metaphor? Surely the word break is inappropriate. In actual fact to break the heart means to burst it open. Anything of any value in our lives needs firstly to be burst open. The child has to burst open from the womb. Spirit bursts from matter. Matter comes from spirit. A chicken bursts open from the egg. We have to burst open the heart in order to feel life. If the heart stays tightly closed, unbroken, unopened, it remains sterile, unfeeling, unearthed, and the intellectual mind overcompensates.

The soul is the great imagination of the creator where we can know our strength, the beauty of our imaginations, our co-creativeness, our inspiration, our insightfulness, our own mercy, our suffering, our loves and hates, our fears. It is also the place where all healing takes place. All our emotions stay locked in the heart and if we dare to express them then the heart expands, our consciousness expands, and a great wave of deep feelings and deep intuitive knowing bursts the chambers of the heart open, and we experience the freshness of our holiness/wholeness. Our earth-minds are stilled into humility. In this place of openness we become aware of the silent presence, or soul presence, in each sentient thing – the cat, the wood in the chair, and the tree in the wood. Looking at the beau-ty of the sky at dawn, we can see our own beauty looking back.

That is how it is to be in life; whatsoever I look upon reflects my inner state. I project my soulfulness out there to meet the universal soul, and if I am not in harmony within myself then I project that wherever I look. My inner state needs to be transformed in order to sense beauty around me. That beauty, and that mercy allows everything to be – stones, grasses, even the cars, shops, animals, and neighbours – without my judgement. All are given their own space to be in the collective family. In this presence, in this consciousness I am allowed to express all that I am, and all that I am is being; the silent witness under any form is being itself. It is as if there is one life and therefore one death, no separation.

The nine blessings of the human being

From the soft earth we receive the gift of flesh
From the bark of the tree - skin
From the roots of the tree - bones
From the water - blood
From the sun - fire
From the moon - feelings
From the seasons - order and structure of life
From all nature - timing and rhythm
And from the flow of life – breath, transformation.

Name the situations that help to burst open your heart either in joy or in pain.

In the past, we have congratulated ourselves in multi-tasking. Now we are asked to concentrate and give our attention to one thing at a time. This helps us stay conscious, and in this way, helps the heart to open. We are learning to see everything and all as a working out of a great mystery, a great creation of which we have the privilege of being a part.

There is a place where pieces of broken hearts go.
There is a mercy that binds them together.
To form the universal heart of compassion
That soothes the heart of another.
– P. Anam-Áire 2005

This idea that when the heart breaks it fragments into pieces, is clearly seen in the above poem. The question is, where does the residual energy of the broken heart go? How is this energy transformed into compassionate care for others? When we dare to split open our hearts over and over, the fragmented energy from our collective splitting fuses together. These ethereal atoms form the universal heart of compassion. Others embarking on the road of opening their hearts will find mercy from the collective consciousness of the active grieving of others. This is the fountain of compassionate love that flows from the great cosmic heart. Until the heart is broken open, love is held captive.

— *Grief* is held captive by the *breath*
— *Breath* is held captive by *anger*
— *Anger* is held captive by *fear*
— Work on your *breath* to get to *grief*
— Work on your *grief* to get to *anger*
— Work on your *anger* to get to *fear*
— Work on you *fear* in order to be *free*
— Choose *freedom* to uncover *love*
— 'Work on' means 'become conscious of'.

Internalizing creation

The Celts believed that before we leave body life the work of the soul was to invite all creation within itself. How can we do this, do we even want to? It is about non-separation; it is about involvement with the world, going deeper and deeper into creation itself, into the animal, plant, mineral worlds without trying to change it, or re-create it in any way. It is about humility, and gratitude, and awe, three great virtues of the soul.

Try the following. Find a space in nature, as near your home as possible. First, begin with the sky, and look at it for five minutes. See the clouds, sun, and moon, if visible. Consciously breathe in and out, three times. Now without trying to change any of it, or judge any of it, become aware of its nature, which is love – divine love. The sky is there because of love. The more we experience 'love', the more we realize how limited our understanding has been. We do not understand how the sky was created; in the same sense, we do not understand love. The images about and around you in the sky will change – a bird might fly by, tops of the trees may hide that part of the sky – but the nature of the sky is unchangeable.

Your nature is also unchangeable. It is this unchangeability of both your natures that connects you. You and sky are one. What does it have to do to be recognized? What does it have to do to be loved? Answer these questions in yourself. Then go to water. If you cannot do so physically, use your imagination. Do the same exercise. Next, observe the animal kingdom: then plants, grasses, and insects. Practise looking without judgement, without preconceived ideas. Now take a flower in your hand, any kind of flower, without rearranging the petals or leaves. Just add your breath to the breath of the flower, and without changing it, be with it.

Now think about somebody you love. Can you do the same exercise? Just be with their nature, without trying to change it. What supports you both in this moment is the nature that you share, and that is divine, and that is love. Can you now go to that person, and share with them the love you feel for them. Now think of somebody you do not like. Do the same exercise, and see if you have changed any of your preconceived ideas. If you have, and you have realized that love supports you both without discrimination, then go to this person and share what you feel. Wisdom is not what I read, nor what I believe, nor what my years are about. Wisdom is about the size of my heart, the measure of my mercy, the heights and breadth of my love, and the length of my arms to embrace another.

NO REGRETS
I'm glad I opened my heart,
Instead of sleeping my dreams.
I'm glad I risked diving deep,
Instead of paddling
In a safe, and shallow stream.
– *P. Anam-Áire* [ix]

Chapter 7

Daily Transformations

What is it to be conscious? How can we live our lives more consciously? These are huge questions, which I can only attempt to answer, not from theory but from the experiences of my own precious life. Somehow, the main difference between living consciously or not is the way I am in relationship with myself, and this naturally gets mirrored in the way I relate to others. When I am being conscious I am more present to the present, and this is the key – the present, this moment. To be truly in the here and now is for us human beings a very difficult challenge. It is about *letting go*. It is about *surrendering*. It is about *not clinging*. It is to be *open* to new possibilities. It is to be more *alive* to our soul's whispers rather than our earth-mind's agendas. It is about *accepting* what is. It is about *self-love*. It is about looking through the eyes of *innocence*. It is about seeing everything as *neutral*. It is about taking *responsibility* for *everything* that happens in my day. And so, it is about living fearlesssly.

> *LOVE BEYOND UNDERSTANDING*
> *True love is born, not from understanding,*
> *But from a willingness to experience all your life.*
> *We have a choice to either try and understand life,*
> *Or surrender to life's heartbreaks and delights.*
> *So many answers we have to know,*
> *So many feelings we dare not show,*
> *So many chances, and we say no.*
> — *P. Anam-Áire*[x]

Falling from grace

In the morning, I can look into the mirror and say welcome to the day Phyllida, and be fully in the moment. I can get to dinnertime and be present with whatever I am doing in a way that is conscious and fulfilling. Dinnertime comes, and I am out of my body time, out of clock time, off on my balloon, into the past or into the future. Why? One phone call does it. The postman does it. It's the dogs' fault. If I hadn't fallen; if I had not bruised my finger, I would still be very conscious! And so, my consciousness, or lack of it, depends on my surroundings. Now I can blame something outside of me for my lack of centredness. When this happens I notice the following physiological changes take place; my breathing is no longer smooth and full. My step is no longer soft upon the earth. My heart beats faster. I try to multitask and I am distracted. I am out of me, and into the environment, which I am judging. I am out of my body, travelling from the past into the future. I am carrying baggage from both places with which to load the present moment. My shoulders pain and my body feels unwell. This affects me psychically, physically, and emotionally. I blame events or others for what is happening. I fall into the role of victim; therefore I have to produce a perpetrator.

Home again

When I return to consciousness again, back to this breath; not back in the past, or dipping into the future, I notice that: my breathing deepens, I slow down, I own the moment, and my contribution to it without judgement. My activities slow down. I am back in me, so the world looks different. I am not as prone to so-called accidents, and I am able to experience my feelings at a deeper level and am able to contain them. It is good to feel the energy of our bodies, and dance the movement coming from within ourselves. As we breathe into every moment, this spontaneous dance can help to ground the rhythms of our bodies in the here and now.

Embodiment *(In-body-meant)*

An arrangement with an earth-mind is made before birth, with the life force or soul aspect whereby the soul, out of love, wills to express itself in the confines of a personality. It joins with the earth-mind in order to ground it in the direction of that arrangement. The soul knows what particular lessons the earth-mind has to experience this time on the earth plane and with enthusiasm, leads it in such a direction. When the arrangements are not adhered to, or when the free will of the earth-mind takes another direction to satisfy the personality, a mistake, or disappointment takes place, and is felt at a soul level, which, subsequently, affects the earth-mind.

When one lifetime has passed, the soul leaves that particular personality and returns to spirit. It rests there until another arrangement to birth is available. Our own soul's wisdom assesses our journeys to earth. There is no God sitting in judgement, determining our life journeys. Three questions our oversoul asks us are: Were there any mistakes or disappointments? Were there many lessons in love learned so that these mistakes could be eradicated? Did the soul give, and receive love? Broken arrangements are not seen as sin or wrongdoings, the soul decides to try again, and again with the help of the body, until eventually, all arrangements, and appointments are kept. This is known as soul actualization, or salvation, or enlightenment.

> **GATHERED INTO LOVE**
> *Did you not know, we are the breath*
> *Flowing from the throat of love?*
> *Did you forget*
> *That we have come to earth the divine*
> *In your heart and mine?*
> — *P. Anam-Áire*[xi]

In Hinduism we read of the churning of the ocean of milk whereby the tug of war between gods and demons produces a thickening, and it is turned into ambrosia. This is a symbol of the stirring of good and evil which is eventually made into supper for the soul.

The first sleep or falling into illusion

The Cauldron teaches that when we come to earth we enter into what is known as *an céad codladh*. This translated means 'the first sleep' or nowadays known as 'entering into depression'. According to the teachings the soul experiences primary grief and this primary grief is the leaving of home – leaving pure, unconditional love to take on the heavy cloak of our humanness. All other grief is secondary; all other grief is simply a reminder of this primary loss, the seeming loss of our innocence, the loss of divine memory, the loss of our true identity. This is the place of homelessness – *gan cara gan companach*. The soul knows that we will not experience this pure love until we leave the body behind, and unite once again with the beloved/spirit. We search for it in vain and are given glimpses when we recognize our own divinity.

What courage it has taken us all to come to earth at this difficult time when we are all being asked to claim this divinity, to stop looking outside our own 'full library of intuitive knowing' for understanding. How often we exchange this treasure for a museum of dead instruction.

Many teachers of spirituality talk about this 'falling from grace' or 'place of forgetting', but they do not call it grief. In Buddhism we are told that when we incarnate, we fall into illusion and continue this illusion until we are enlightened. According to Celtic Consciousness, we all have between five and seven chances to reincarnate in the same lifetime. Every time we make a complete leap of belief or transform our thinking so radically, as to seem to be a completely new person, we enter into another incarnation. Illness can be a place of radical transformation for people which can lead to open loving acceptance of their lives, and everyone around them.

If you reflect the many times you have made real paradigm shifts of consciousness from one set of beliefs to another, you may understand this teaching. No doubt as we get older we change our thinking on many issues, but we are talking about real shifts, real transformations, which involve experiencing those little deaths in daily living. Enlightenment has been described by many spiritual writers as a state of non-duality, where we know who we are, and see the illusive nature of everything around us. It suggests full involvement whilst remaining unattached. This is where the difficulty arises.

In life yet detached

Brigit says:

Live every breath,
Sing loudly your song of greeting to all,
Then give it away to the wind.

Seemingly I have the ability to live each breath consciously. I can sing my song loudly, which suggests a great joy in sharing my life with all creation, and then I can let go of the song. I let the wind carry it away as I am not attached to it. So many things even in one breath distract us. Therefore meditation or being with nature are helpful in bringing us back to our awareness, awareness of our breath, the source of life in us.

How many of us really sing our life-song? I believe this does not necessarily mean actually singing, rather it suggests an outreach into life, a projection of our healed selves/souls into the world. How many of us are living our Soul's potential? This word *loudly* is important as it challenges us to be heard. It challenges us to give a blessing or greeting to others, and to share our particular gifts with all creation. It does not suggest withdrawing from life. Rather it asks us to go even deeper into life, deeper into the world, and interact with all beings. It is in the world of human beings that we are challenged, that we can be aware of our wounds from the past, and it is in the world of human beings that we can heal our lives. For this we have come into the earth. How difficult it is for us at times to be fully in the world of matter, and yet not of it, to have our own sense of motivation, our own meaning to life, our own integrity. Unattachment does not mean uninvolvement. It means that I do not give my soul for it, therefore, I do not suffer when I and it are separate.

INSIDE OUT
I live my life from the inside out, I love like I've never been forsaken.
I carry my fears to the edge of their doubt, I dance like I've never
been broken.
I have come from the home of belonging, pitched my tent in the house
of illusion,

Where I traded the truth of all ages for the lies and disguise of religion.
I had forgotten the reason I came here. In a maze of confusion I stumbled.
Though my mind tried to find me some answers they were found on the ground of experience.
I live my life from the inside out, I laugh like I've never known grieving.
I carry my fears to the edge of their doubt, I give because I'm always receiving.
— *P. Anam-Áire* [xii]

The seven incarnations

The first incarnation of spirit in a soul seed was in the place of *abred* – 'lower earth'. In the Eastern tradition it is the place of the first chakra or energy centre called *muladhara*. This is the place of earthing, and the colour is brown-red. It is the place of struggle for survival, learning to be human with still all the animal instincts, a joyless existence. The body was not totally upright, and the arms were heavy by our sides. It was a time of getting to know the body and its functions. It was taught that this first teaching was simply to survive the stress of body heaviness, and dense matter, and go through the human birth and dying process. Earth-mind was the emphasis. Protection of what was mine was all-important.

The second incarnation took place in *gwynfred* – 'lower earth', or second chakra called *svadisthana*. This is the place of reproduction and sexuality, and the colour is orange-red. This was the place of self-pleasuring, and there was more interaction with others but as yet not in an altruistic way. Again territory and possessions were important, as was control over others. The heart did not open yet, and many times we killed for spite and revenge.

The third incarnation took place in *neart*, or third chakra called *manipura*, a place of transition, a place of crossroads. This is the place of the sun energy where power, me-first syndrome, fear, greed, action, and reaction dwelt. The colour was a yellow-orange. As *neart* also means centre, it represented the centre of the body. Here it was said the soul dwelt mostly, and sent messages to the rest of the body to awaken.

The fourth incarnation took place in *croian* – 'upper earth', which in Sanskrit is the *anahata* chakra. This is the place of the heart of feelings, but sometimes can be over-emotional. The body was now opening to the soul from the solar plexus. Caring for others and sharing what we had were our important lessons in this incarnation, learning to love in a less possessive way. Feeling relatedness to all life was also an opening to the heart of all. It is also known as the place of the 'warrior of the heart'. The colour here is green.

The fifth incarnation took place in *guth* –, known as *vissudi* in Sanskrit. This is the place of creativity and service to others, the place of deep joy and appreciation for all life, a willingness to become more and more conscious in life, and a consciousness of death. The colour is blue-green. It is also the place or passageway from the head to the heart.

The sixth incarnation took place in *cengant* or *anja* chakra, the place of intuitive knowing; the place of bliss and of joyful expansion into all love. This is the place of royalty. The colour is magenta. The soul's journey is all-important, and the dear earth-mind has been loved into the heart. This is also the place of the teacher, the one who shows the way, and is conscious that s/he is also on the way home to soul.

The seventh incarnation takes place in *ceannard*, or *sahasrara* chakra. This incarnation is where oneness with spirit takes place. It is the place of internal marriage of soul and spirit. Service to others is the only reason for incarnating this time. We have no unfinished business to take care of, and it is our joy to release others into joy. This is the place of the high king and queen, the crowning place.

The eighth, ninth and tenth incarnations were places of pure ecstacy. Such beings were said to be the guiding lights of the oversoul and have more to do with divine beingness than earthedness as they hovered between all the worlds. Collective divine emanations from all created phenemona was said to be gathered by these beings, and by this gathering souls in distress in other worlds were helped.

Paradigm shifts of consciousness are attainable for us all, and changing rapidly from one set of beliefs to another, from one life pathway to another, are not only probabilities but a possibility. The more conscious we become, the more our bodies will accelerate in their vibration vortexes. This no doubt affects the nervous system, and we need to be more caring of our physical bodies at such times of radical catharsis. The soul is forever urging us in the direction of the crown, but it will not interfere or push us. It will remind us with many little nudges and as Hannah says, 'with mighty big shoves'

Helpmates on our journey

The Celts believed in the spirit world, and its willingness to help us on our journeys to our Soul's rest. The Christian Church carried on this belief, in particular the Catholic belief. Angels and archangels, together with saints and holy departed were known as the main helpmates of souls in earth. The communion of all saints was also a means of help. It is believed in the Catholic Church that a special guardian angel came to earth with us to be our own guide through life. This so-called being of light, with a knowing beyond our intellect has one task to do, and that is to look after us humans.

The Celts held their 'other worldly' help in great honour. In particular when there were community disputes, the help of other worlds was called upon and a place was kept vacant in the circle for such. They were called upon to help with the harvest, to name children, and to settle feuds amongst neighbours. These guests were always addressed before any one spoke, and a long breath space was given during which time no one could interrupt. My Nanny always invited the spirit people to the table when we ate together. The chair was put there for them, and no one could sit on it! These spirit people were referred to as *duine aoifa* – 'the holy ones'. It was believed that at birth and death these unseen guests came to assist humans. At birth their task was to re-echo the note that enticed the soul to earth. It was believed that the same angel or helper re-echoed the same note in a higher octave when the soul departed the body.

There was also a belief that the good deeds we did as human beings formed entities that materialized into helpmates. It was said when we die, these entities went before us, and prepared a beautiful place of welcoming. One of the joys of entering spirit life after body life was being shown the good energy we had left behind on the earth, thus, helping in the evolution of souls still there. These beings were personified so that children could better identify with them, and so fairies and angels with wings came into being. Naturally, the same could be said for the dark thoughts that formed entities of darkness, or devils. 'They roam around us trying to bring us down', my Nanny would say, with a shake of her head. This enticed us to be good, to do good acts, and attract only good fairies, not the goblins, or mischievous devils.

This other-worldly guidance is also about tough love. The angel guide is here to reheart us of the contract we made before embodying, and they are not at all emotionally involved with us. They love in a detached way. This way, and this way alone can they be of help and assistance. If we have pre-arranged to attain enlightenment this time our angel with the help of our souls will lovingly help us to use situations that will ensure that we learn our particular lesson.

Shadow angel

The shadow angel was just as important as the light one, for indeed one was seen as the counterpart of the other. Therefore no judgement was made of it. The Christian Church however discriminated and the light angel was deemed the helper of man therefore good; and the dark angel was the destroyer of man therefore bad or evil. Later the shadow angel was named devil by the Christian Church. Lucifer was a so-called good light angel in the beginning, and later having had a dispute with God, he was named bad, and dark. He was punished for his rebelliousness, and condemned to the lower regions of earth. It was said that he wandered the earth destroying souls. (As if the souls could be annihilated!)

The story of Adam and Eve would seem to suggest that a similar thing happened to them in the Garden of Eden. It would appear that the God of the Christian Church did not like opposition and needed to be obeyed. Any autonomous or self-directed behavior by His creation was punished, and independent choice was not tolerated. Adam and Eve had disobeyed the Father, and were sent from the Garden of Eden (*nirvanha*) to earth to live in pain and suffering all their days. If you disobey, you have to suffer. The son was unable to rebel therefore he stayed the child in his relationship to his father. Always having to obey and bow to the Father's wishes, prevents the young man from growing up, from self authority and autonomy.

Chapter 8

Natural Rhythms
or Order
(Ordú Nádúrtha)

The tribe

The tribe is a continuation of family, a community built upon the hand-ing down of traditions, customs, and rituals. Each tribe has its own set of values, its own regulations, which must not be broken. When these rules are broken by a member of the tribe, punishment ensues in the form of public humiliation, negative insinuation, passive aggression, or isolation. Whilst regulations are necessary and important, rigid standards are often imposed, and handed down without thought of individuation or care for the soul. The so-called rim walker needs to break out of these controls, and find another reality if needs be. That other reality may, or may not, be known to ourselves. We only know we have to leave home and to rebel. Later on we need to reclaim our power, remember, recall our pro-jections, reconcile, regain inner authority, and bring the blessing of who we are back to the tribe. We are never the same again.

Have you left your tribe?

Have you left your tribe in any of the following etc. belief systems?
- *Religion*
- *Relationships – marriage*
- *Sexuality*

- *Children*
- *Attitude towards money*
- *Roles of male/female and children*
- *Politics*
- *Work ethics*
- *Health and medicines*
- *Authority*
- *Choice of profession*

Before leaving the tribe in Celtic times, permission had to be granted by the grandfather. The elders listened carefully without judgement, and usually the young person was able to leave with a blessing, but not before they were initiated into a ritual of leaving the father's house. Six tasks were necessary. They had to:

- *State why they wanted to leave.*
- *Ask forgiveness from the ancestors.*
- *Ask for the father's blessing.*
- *Thank their mother for giving them life.*
- *Ask for the goodwill of their siblings.*
- *Tell the community.*

When considering life today, it is clear that none of these orders are fully adhered to. What price do we pay for this lack of consciousness? Individuation is an important part of maturity. Indeed, an essential component. Do you still adopt tribal values as your own? What tribal values serve you today? Tribal customs and rituals are not all negative. Do not throw out the baby with the bath water. Have you ever experienced alienation, shaming, or emotional blackmail because you would not adhere to a tribal belief? How did you respond at the time, even if it was 'for your own good'? How would you respond today? How does one actually take leave from the tribe? How may one leave behind the old ways and take on a new credo, of which one is still not clear, of which only the soul has knowledge?

In many ways the rim walker is not interested in the 'how' of it all, or indeed, why she feels the way she does. Her only concern is a deep inner knowing that the time for change has come. The time for transformation has come. The time to leave the house of the mother has come. It is time to find herself her real heart self, under the ashes of her own burning. The rim walker knows about timing, listens to her inner rhythms, and knows only that the external rhythms are alien. She has to break the rules, and rebel with compassion. She has to go deeper and deeper into the world of not knowing, with her only guide being her inner knowing, leading the way.

In Celtic Consciousness it is important to ask forgiveness from the tribe before we leave. When I left the Catholic Church in 1983, I left with anger. Years later I realized that the anger was interfering with the choices I was making, and so I had to somehow reach the stage of forgiveness, and only then could I be free. This I did in 1996 when in a small ritual I let go of religious abuse, and forgave myself for carrying such rage. Now I feel free to go into a Catholic Church, light a candle, and give thanks. All has been stirred into acceptance of my own precious incarnation.

Coupling *(Lechéile)*

The teachings hold that every living organism has within it innate sacred order, balance, and equanimity. When these are not adhered to or respected, disorder and disharmony ensues. One of the laws of nature is that of the attraction of opposites, for without this attraction and consequential fusion, nothing can come into being. The nature of life is to attract. The nature of death is to repel which is not negative. The Celtic beliefs around 'coupling' or *lechéile* are in accordance with the natural order, so the human male and female species may get together if they choose, in answer to the magnetic call of their souls. It was believed that when two people feel an attraction for one another each soul emits their own personal sound, and if these sounds are in harmony, then spiritual love flows between them. If there is no harmony, then the love was of the body only, and would not stand the windstorms of life together. This attraction builds in its intensity as they get to know each other, and they cohabit. It is important however, that the couple have the blessing of both parents before they do so. In some countries even today the man asks the father's permission to marry his daughter.

There is an underlying rank and order within the family setting, which albeit, though rarely outwardly acknowledged as such, still governs human behaviourism. It is clear to see this order in nature. The seasons have their particular orderly sequence, and it is evident that each season has its own role. The animal kingdom respects the fundamental rules of participating in life in earth, and treats with aggression another animal that disobeys the inner code. We will concentrate however on order within the human family.

Relationships

Sexuality was synonymous with spirituality; therefore, it was deemed sacred. Sexuality between persons of the same sex was known as *aonacht* or 'one form' sex, and this was accepted in the psychology and spirituality of creative development. It could be said that the *aonacht* were mostly artists, designers, or storytellers. Their psyche and physical make-up were more feminine than their male counterparts. Most of the *seabhéans* ('holy women') were very in tune with their psychic powers, and their sexuality gave them the power, the earth power to transcend gender. They were considered as holy and in touch with the divine order of things. *Aonacht* was not looked upon as extraordinary or unnatural, but seen as part of the divine, and therefore spiritual.

It was the Christian Church that used the word 'sinner' in association with the word homosexual. Even today homosexual men are not welcomed in the Catholic Church for ordination. These self-professed Christian homosexual men are ostracized not because of their willingness to serve, but because of their sexuality.

When a couple, male and female, usually around 14 or 15 years of age, were attracted to one another they were instructed by the education council regarding the sexual rites of passage. Usually the men taught the males, and the women taught the females. Underlined is how the instructions took place.

According to the teachings, after the couple decide to continue the relationship, the next stage is that they get to know each other through the four seasons. If they can still find a reason to be together through the cold and dark of winter, through the bursting forth of passion and intensity of spring, through the long gathering days and nights of summer, and on through the transformational changing moods of autumn, they then naturally make a communal ritual. We call this engagement. The couple is now known in the community as partners, *lechéile*, and are treated as such. They now have the protection and support of the community. Older members help them to make their nest amongst them. They are no longer available for another lover or partner, and they exchange and display some kind of body adornment, necklace, ring, tattoo or body markings in order to communicate this. (In parts of Ireland and Scotland, they wear the *claddagh* ring – two hearts cradled in two hands.) They remain 'engaged' or 'betrothed' for another four seasons, enduring the changes and ambivalences of their own inner feelings.

At the end of that winter they take time away from each other – three days and three nights – to ask their souls the questions they need to ask. They believed the answers would come from nature, whose business it was to maintain and sustain order, and help humans find it. When they come together the male asks his beloved if she will be his *bean ceile* or 'wife' and be by his side until they die. This is the ultimate union of earth-mind and soul, represented in the form of male and female. This is the *heiros gamus* – the 'sacred union'. If the female answers yes the community witnesses the next ordered stage in their relationship, which we call marriage. It was known as 'hand fasting' or *laimhe ceile* in the old tradition. When the answer was no, the community again was asked to witness the *dul amach* – 'separation'. Each person leaves the home they had cohabited and says goodbye. If the female was very young she returned to the house of her mother.

If a couple chose to separate they did not meet during a full cycle of the moon. This was to give them time to adjust to being alone again, and find themselves again. I believe that when we have been sexually engaged with another person we create a bond that is not released when we part. At an energetic level the ties are still unbroken until one or other, or better both of them decide to release them.

Releasing sexual ties

The following is a way whereby that may be achieved. If the two people who have been involved decide to do the ritual together they need to meet, and light a small tea-light candle each, in the company of a witness. Standing facing each other they say: 'I (name) release you, (naming the other) from the residue of sexual energy connected with our time together. I thank you for the love we shared, and I set you free to be with another and be happy.' When this is done they blow out each other's candle, and offer the candle for burning on an open fire, or if there is no fire they give the candles to someone to burn for them. They then give each other a blessing, for example, 'I bless you with joy and courage.' or whatever.

They then take the hand of the other and say thank you, and part, going in opposite directions. If only one person engages in the ritual it is done in the following way: Light two candles, and have a witness to your ritual. Holding one candle in your hand place the other on the floor in front of you, some distance from you. Stand facing the candle and repeat the words of release as above: 'I, (name) release you...' When you have finished bless the other person, and burn the candles, then say goodbye. Stay a while in silence, and then leave the place. This is a way of blessing the time you spent together, and releasing yourself and the other. You are both now free to love again, and be sexual again when the time is right without the intrusiveness of sexual energy of the past relationship.

Responsibility of parenting

The natural order for a married partnership was that if the couple were young enough, they naturally had children. If they were not physically fit, and well, they took herbs, given to them by the medicine woman, and so birth was prevented. It was believed that physical fitness was important if a couple wanted to conceive. If the couple were infertile they took on the children of other families to rear and love. This was known as *ag leanbh-aire* – 'child caring'. It was later called 'good parenting' or 'godparents'. If they did not take on a child to rear, they worked together with a project of a kind, which was usually something creative. At the end of the day instead of being with the children, the women sewed and 'sprigged' (embroidered) and the men may have worked with clay, glass blowing, or carpentry etc. Later on this became what we now know in Ireland as 'home industry'. A song explains the closeness of such enterprises:

> At the end of the day, when the sun burns the sky,
> Will you sit here with me before we lie?
> Will you colour the cloth green red and gold,
> While I whistle gently the clay to mould
> For no child have we to play at our knee,
> Only our sweet love keeps us company.
> — P. Anam-Áire

It was important that the couple contributed to the community in whatever way they could. Having children was naturally the highest service, for it maintained the continuity of the tribe or clan, and that was essential. If a couple decided to continue a partnership without the ceremony of hand fasting, it was frowned upon as it was not in keeping with the natural order of life. Their relationship did not have the blessing from the ancestors, and would be difficult. It was said that the curse of the fathers came upon the sons, and they were not successful in their work. Ill health was visited upon the female partner, if through selfish reasons she would not bear a child, and as she grew older, a dullness of spirit set in as she mourned for long times alone, nowadays known as depression. Seemingly souls wanting to come to earth were disappointed, and she heard their cries. Now she was too old to conceive.

It is clear that the elders believed in the sacred order of life, and adhered to this order as much as possible, so that harmony and good humour should abound within the community. If a couple did have children, they were attended to with care, and great love. Children were seen as a gift from the Great Mother, and were appreciated as such. Mothers would not have dreamt of leaving the home to go to work, leaving the child with a stranger. If mother had to go away on her own for a while, the *Mathair Mór*, or grandmother took care of the children. The extended family cared for all children as there own. Fathers and grandfathers were just as involved with this caring as mothers.

The ordered role of father was very important, as it was his privilege to provide for mother and children. He took his role seriously and worked hard to care for their temporal needs. Mother had another role for she was known as the first teacher of the child, and as such was honoured. The role of the grandparents was very important also; as they handed down the stories, and the wise ways of the tribe to their grandchildren, and were treated with great respect by them.

May the love and honour of your ancestors go with you, and may you always hear the small still voice of their wisdom in you, inviting you to go deeper and deeper into life.

Male initiation

The male was taken to 'The House of Men' and three of the older men gave him the verbal lessons in sexual behaviour to benefit himself and his partner. As nothing sacred was written down, and no books were available, the young male listened very carefully. He was asked if he understood everything, and was questioned on the lesson if he answered in the affirmative. If he said he did not understand everything, he was taught the whole lesson all over again. Thus it was until he knew all the lessons. Sometimes the lessons took all day, sometimes only a few hours.

In the instructions he was shown a picture of the female body that one of the elders had just drawn, and he was taught the various pleasure areas. It was up to him to gently, and with deep awareness activate them into pleasure. He was instructed how to give his partner the utmost joy in her body, and how to really be in joy himself. It was believed that when a man gave a woman, his partner, joy in her body, then he was pleasing the great goddess and gained her blessings thereby. As the couple was *lechéile* ('engaged') and would, within the next year, be ready for 'hand fasting', contraception was taught and this took the form of herbs and various potions given by the medicine man or woman in the community. Body control methods were also used and breathing techniques shown to the young man, ways by which he could control the emission of the precious seed of life without stress.

Female initiation

The young woman was also instructed in the ways of sexual pleasure. This she was taught by the older women in 'The House of Women'. She went through a similar procedure, at the end of which the young couple met and, with the help and support of the older members, were blessed and celebrated. This time of being together was known as 'breathing the fire'. It is possible that this meant that they were now beginning to understand what passion and 'being as close as breath' meant. When the Church created the separation between sexuality and spirituality, it created not only discrimination and inequality amongst the sexes; it also created judgements and condemnations of women.

When the goddess, *Sheila-na-gig*, visited the earth plane, it was said that she taught the women how to give themselves sexual pleasure, and it was said that good health and longevity were the results. Women were taught to pleasure themselves and to enjoy each other's bodies as the body of the goddess. Rituals of braiding each other's hair, and massaging each other's bodies were deemed holy and blessed. This was a natural way for woman to celebrate, and get to know there own bodies, and the bodies of other women. Woman gathered together and delighted in their storytelling, some blatantly sexual in contents. Laughter, chants, and stories filled the large chamber as women discussed child rearing, making food, men, and their sexual and blessed ceremonies.

They created many rituals around their menstruation and handed these ceremonies to the younger women for them to continue – the monthly flow was not flushed away like it is today. It was ceremoniously taken from the vagina in a small shell, and placed in the earth. A blessing was said as the earth covered the red blood from the woman's womb. The full moon was not particularly celebrated by Celtic women; it was however a double blessing for the young woman if her menstruation came at full moon. The energy of the moon was said to fill her womb with a longing to procreate. If this happened to a young woman who had a partner, she was more inclined to want to be pregnant at that time than any other. She was said to be 'full of the moon'.

It was an unspoken rule amongst the women that they never show their genitals in public places. Women's genitals were looked upon as sacred hidden place of grace, and therefore had to be treated as such. Many women believed that in giving this grace away they dishonoured the goddess who asked them to 'keep your treasure house covered as you do the chalice on your altar'. Men honoured this injunction. No doubt, when they were making love this did not apply. It was more the general decorum in the day-to-day affairs. The chalice or cauldron was treated with honour and respect. It held within its walls the sacred juice of creation and creativity.

Preparation for parenthood

When the potential parents felt that the time was right to procreate, they approached different wise people in the community to advise and support them. These wise people were usually the astrologer, the oldest Druid, the wise woman, the most creative bard, and the ovate. They advised from their particular discipline. If the couple proceeded they were told when the most beneficial time would be to conceive, and they took all the advice to make sure everything was in order in the universe to assist them.

Male initiation before fathering

When a couple decided they would like to procreate, preparations had to be made before the birth. The father had a very important job to do. It was easy for them to discern whether the child was male or female, and he knew the special work he had to do if the child was male. This entailed much psychological healing of his father's line. If the pending father had not received his father's blessing he had to rectify this before the birth of his own son because that would affect the newborn. Often that was the reason given when a male child did not come at the expected time. It was thought that the male child could not come happily into a family that did not keep this tribal belief. With a female child, the mother had to make sure her feelings and dealings with her mother were friendly, otherwise she had to work on making it so. If a female child did not come at the expected time of birth, it meant that the expectant mother did not agree with her mother, and so the child was reluctant to come. Nowadays it would be unheard of to suggest that a delay in the delivery date of a child was due to the parents not having received their parent's blessing!

If for some reason the male had not received the father's blessing, he had to go to him and talk about it. One of the reasons a young man did not get the blessing was because he married a woman with whom the father did not agree. Another reason might be that he did not get the father's permission before starting a craft unworked at before by any of his ancestors and by so doing scorned the old ways. He may have rejected his father's advice about something. Whatever the reason, it was absolutely essential that he made at-one-ment with the father, and so received the blessing. It seems that good psychology was at work here. Nowadays people attend all sorts of seminars and workshops dealing with the disorder in their lives, and try to heal the dysfunctional family tree.

> *The son that has his Father's blessing*
> *Can travel to the top of the mountain*
> *And from there his light will shine.*
> — *P. Anam-Áire*

And again, regarding the daughter:

> *The daughter that has her Mother's blessing*
> *Is able to go forward without crying or sorrow.*
> — *P. Anam-Áire*

Naming the child

The father names the child and welcomes it. The idea being that the father calls the life force to embody and it is he who names it. The name is spoken three times into the child's left ear, and both father and mother sing it to the child. The community joins in chanting the name. Later on, when the child goes on their chosen life quest, they will be given a name by a wise man to take them into the next stage of their life. Naming is important because the vibrations in each letter carry a strong energy for the child's life. The father holds the child, breathes on its face so that the child gets to know the different texture of mother's and father's skin, the male touch, and the female touch. Then he prays 'My mouth on your doorway my soul kisses yours. Great Spirit speaks your name; I carry it to your ears.'

Protecting the child

As in most ancient cultures skins of animals were reserved for clothing, and for the warm covering of the children. If a child was ill, an animal skin was draped in such a way that it covered the child's body completely, and so it was said that the spirit animal kept watch over the child. Daily the people gave thanks for the life of the animal, and it was believed that the soul of the animal would return to the earth plane as a healer. The child who had the animal skin as its protector thus, was said to have extra gifts of healing, and was watched over by that particular animal for as long as he/she lived. Many stories were told about gifted children; most of whom were healed from diseases by the animal skin.

> Brother animal your Soul at rest,
> Your strong Spirit wakened by the fire in your breast,
> With the sense of the Gods, and a love so strong,
> You cradle the little one back to her soul.

Teaching the child

As the child grew, she/he learned the way of the clan. Most instruction was in the form of stories. Gradually, children added to these stories and so it was that many versions of one story were told. Children were encouraged to do so as it was a way of activating their powers of creativity and imagination. It was said that when one sits in a circle of others that a story longs to be told. All that was needed was for one person to open their heart to the story, and it would flow from the mouth of their soul. The storyteller had to surrender to the spirit of the story asking to be told. She/he had no attachment as to how the story would go. The ending was not important, just the telling of it. Many stories did not want an ending, but it asked that the teller should experience the ending in their life, and then tell it to the others later, even years later. This is how the word 'mystery' got its name, literally 'my-story', and each person telling a story had their own particular ending. Many stories only ended at the death of the storyteller. Of course, psychologically speaking, everyone tells their own story.

People's own unfulfilled longings and unconscious shadow stories got told as the storyteller dared to surrender to the inner ghost of the story. It was believed that whoever dared to tell stories of raging gods and goddesses were relieved of their own 'thunder in the liver'. This is sound psychology; when we express the story, and sound the anger in a safe environment, it does not affect us negatively. The witnessing of our heart's pain heals it. Stories of love and delight, of lovers reuniting, were all aspects of deep longing from within the teller of the story. In the story personal dramas and traumas were healed.

Chapter 9

Sacred Celtic Calendar

These are the eight Celtic festivals:

- New Year – 31 October
- Winter Solstice – 21 December
- Brigit's Day – 2 February
- Spring Equinox – 21 March
- Beltane (or *Bealtaine*) – 1 May
- Summer Solstice – 21 June
- Harvest – 31 July–1 August
- Autumn Equinox – 21 September

The four main celebrations are:

- *Samhain* (pronounced sawain) – 31 October-1 November
- *Imbolg* (pronounced imbolig) – 1-2 February
- *Bealtaine* (pronounced balchinny) – 1 May (originally 13 May)
- *Lughnasa* (pronounced lunasa) – 31 July-1 August

Samhain

Samhain is a blessed time in the Catholic Church for remembering the dead. It is called 'All Souls'. It was a time set aside for going to church, and praying certain prayers for the souls who were lingering in that place of suffering called purgatory before going to heaven. Babies who died without having received the sacrament of baptism went to a place of beauty and happiness called limbo. They allegedly would never see the face of God. Celtic Christians believed that the departed souls could be released into heaven through the intervention of prayers and fastings. They in turn having reached heaven would keep an eye out for us when our time came. Fair is fair! This belief was carried on by the Catholic Church alone. It has kept the love of ritual and colourful ceremony alive in my psyche and has provided a rich and deep foundation for my involvement in Celtic Consciousness. The Catholic Church also taught a firm belief in the other worlds of creation. The absorbent mind of the child in me silently observed the many treasures that were to be found in sacred ceremonies such as Nanny McDyre performed at *Samhain*.

I remember the great care she took to make sure bread and tea were left out for the souls on 'All Hallows Night' or 'All Holy Night', which as we know became 'Halloween'. She went around the house flicking holy water at the four corners, at the ceiling and out by the threshold of the door. This was done to welcome the good or god spirits and to keep out any mischievous ones that might be seeking refuge. I well recall her words:

> *In the name of Brigit of the hearth,*
> *I send you on your way, if you be up to no good.*
> *In the name of Brigit with her sword,*
> *I send her after you.*
> *In the name of Brigit of the green cloak,*
> *I ask her to guide you, if you be bringing a blessing.*

She would end her incantations with the sign of the cross on her own body and then say,

> *Jesus and Brigit and Mary*
> *Have mercy on the poor souls in purgatory*
> *And give them rest. Amen.*

She would then smile to herself, make a cup of strong tea with *uisge beatha* (the Gaelic word for 'whiskey' or 'water of life'), sit down by the open fire, and make some deep throaty sighs up the chimney. I loved the way she would sit so contentedly, and nod her 'ayes' into the flames. Her name was Annie Brigit, my mother's name was Brigit Agnes and my aunt's name was Brigit, too. Brigit was a household name in many Irish Catholic families. After a while, when the night was dark, and the light from the fire cast its eerie shadows into the kitchen, the neighbours would come to visit. Somehow, they knew that Nanny would have her wee (as in small) cups of holy water, and they always liked to share a cup or two with her on this special holy night. One night she left a cup of the holy water for the souls to enjoy. Imagine her surprise in the morning when she found it had been drunk. The miracle was talked about for some time. I didn't tell the truth until I was grown up! I have never been one for whiskey since!

All Souls Night was a time for contacting the dead. Somehow, it was accepted that the souls, that had not long left the earth plane, could be easily contacted as if they were in a waiting chamber, waiting to be directed elsewhere. I believe that some clairvoyants and mediums have developed their psychic gifts due to childhood traumas, of which many are unaware.

According to Celtic teachings those who leave the earth with little development of their consciousness, but who have never the less lived good lives as far as they were able, still function in the spirit world from their astral bodies. By that I mean they do not travel far from the earth plane, and so are easily contacted. They live out similar lives to the ones they had just lived on earth, and by our prayers, and their willingness to learn, can travel deeper into pure consciousness. Souls who have widened their consciousness while in body life are not accessible but may themselves materialize if needs be – Jesus on the road to Emmaus, the Virgin Mother in her appearance to the children at Fatima and Lourdes. My grandmother used to say that her brother used to feel very near after the first year of departure, but not after that. There are many mansions in the house of god, and so we all go to the mansion that fits our consciousness.

It was a custom also in the Catholic Church on the 2 November to pray to the saints who had died. This was called 'All Saints Day'. I have a memory of asking for Saint Brigit's help in times of illness and distress. Many people wore a linen cloth around their middle, having had it blessed by a holy woman in the name of Brigit. We were not told anything about the goddess, Brigit. That would have been heresy and possibly a 'mortal sin', as she would have been classified as a 'false god', and a female one into the bargain!

A ritual of letting go

This ritual of letting go can be done on one's own. Sit in nature, or in a comfortable position on a chair, and with your eyes closed, feel your breath. Without changing the rhythm, notice how you breathe in, and you breathe out. Now begin to exaggerate the rhythm, becoming mindful of a longer inhalation, and a longer exhalation. Five counts for in breath and five for the out breath. Continue this for the next five breaths, noticing the body relaxing more and more as you do so. Now become aware that there is pause after the in breath, and after the out breath; a natural time of inactivity of space, of void, of total passivity. Exaggerate the pausal time between in breath and out breath, say to the count of three. Notice within yourself any changes this has brought about in your psyche. Continue breathing thus for the next five breaths. To summarize: Breathe in five counts. Hold three counts. Breathe out five counts. Hold out three counts. Keep relaxing more, and more as you go deeper into this rhythm for another count of five breaths. Now become aware of the natural breath without counting. Let the body breathe itself and relax.

Now imagine that the past year of your life is in front of you, containing all your experiences, all the choices, all the outcomes, all the responsibilities, a potpourri of your life for the past twelve months; a time you will never have again, a time that is dead, and needs to be buried. This past year needs much from you in this moment, so that it may have a happy death, and a joyful resurrection into a new life.

Burial of the past year

If already not in nature, go into nature and find something that represents the whole of the last twelve months. Bring it to your altar. Light a candle. Burn incense. Put a picture of you in front of the candle. Kneel down in front of it. Say the following words: 'I thank you life for having given me so many opportunities in which I had choice to react or respond. I ask forgiveness for the times when I chose to react. I ask forgiveness of my own soul, for the mistakes I made that brought pain and sadness to me, and those around me. I let go now of any guilt or shame attached to these choices. I ask forgiveness from the universe.'

Taking the artifact from nature, representing the past twelve months, hold it in the palm of your hands and breathe on it, and say these words: 'As I lived these months I now let them go, and ask life herself not to remember my ungratefulness, and my lack of integrity. May these past twelve months be blessed and transformed as I now lay them down. As winter turns to spring I allow this artifact to go deep into the earth, to die and so to live, so that I may also die, and take up new life in spring.' Now take the artifact and go into nature. Holding it in your left hand, scrape up the earth with your right hand, and with these words, drop the artifact into the earth: 'I give thanks for these past twelve months. I am forgiven all mistakes. May life be in me, and transform what needs to be transformed. Seá.'

Now place the earth over the artifact, bow to it, and leave. Come back into the house, again go to your altar, take the photograph of yourself, breathe three times on it, and say the following words: 'As I continue to breathe life, I continue to make choices. May I enjoy the consequences of the choices I make in the next twelve months, so that grace, joy, and love may attend me. May all creation be blessed thrice because of this sacred ritual. Seá.

Imbolg

Celebrated on 2 February, *Imbolg* was the Celtic feast of light and new life. It was celebrated as the first day of the spring equinox. It seems that nature woke from her slumber to have a look around! Brigit the goddess is said to have spoken to the trees, and with her warm breath enticed the buds to awaken and shoot into life. It was a time of glad tidings as the long, long days of dark winter were soon to end, and Brigit, like Persephone, would walk the fields and skip and dance through the meadows whilst singing the whole of nature awake. The following words I attribute to Brigit:

She wakens from slumber the buds on the tree,
She flings a new song to the birds on the wing,
She lengthens and lengthens the days dull and cold,
And breathes to us softly, a mild southern wind.
— *P. Anam-Áire*

A ritual or preparation for the light was one of great merriment and song. On 1 February the community would gather around the fire, and ask if a story needed telling. They did not rehearse or learn any of the songs or stories. The teller himself/herself did not know how it would end, or indeed how it would begin. Bards, who were of high renown in the community, were much respected for they held the magick of words.

The Catholic Church in Ireland celebrates the death of Saint Brigid on 2 February. It was called *la fheile Brigid*. On the night before *Imbolg*, we as children made 'Saint Brigid crosses', which represented the cross of Jesus. (This symbol initially represented the wheel of life or the four directions, rather than the cross.) They were hand woven with rushes from the fields that had been dried near the hearth fire. It was said that the house that carried such a cross would have no harm come to it or the inhabitants, nor would any of the family suffer from a terrible plague. This custom of making Brigid crosses is still taught in many schools in Ireland today.

In pre-Christian times crosses were also made from rushes depicting and honouring the four elements of fire, water, air, and earth. The centre of the cross, which was an intricate square, was woven to represent a mandala of beauty and complexity. It represented the centre or *neart* – the 'source of all life', the 'giver of breath'. The celebrating of life was endemic in the heart of the Celts and in many of the Irish.

The cross was also seen as the crossing or the *trasna* – 'the place where decisions have to be made and routes have to be taken'. It is the place of transformation and change. Jesus was at the *trasna* on Calvary; he was at the place of transformation, the place of the skull or *golgotha*. The skull represented the death of the flesh, but the belief was that the life force or soul transmigrated, and came back at another time to continue *mo scéal* – 'my story'.

How do you celebrate your life at this time in the year? Do you give thanks for the light that never goes out in you? It may be of benefit to consider doing a ritual with some friends at this time, the beginning of springtime.

A ritual for *Imbolg*

Each person taking part in the ritual collects something from nature that symbolizes a habit, a trait or dysfunctioning behaviour they wish to let go of. A typical nature gift for the fire could be a fir cone, a dead leaf, or a dead piece of bark from a tree. They also consider what virtue they need to support their willingness to change at this time. The women then gather dry rushes and twigs, whilst the men gather the bigger branches and sticks. When the gathering is done they stand in a circle all together, and lay down their firewood in front of them. Whoever is guiding the ritual blesses the circle, known as casting the circle, and goes around the outside chanting or praying a prayer of blessing and protection. She may invite in all the ancestors to witness the ceremony. She then joins the circle herself and welcomes everyone, and offers a prayer, chants, or plays a drum. The fire is then constructed in the following way.

The women each having consciously decided what it is they wish to change in their life, and what gift they will take from the flames comes forward. They lay down twigs and small sticks to form a circle. When the last woman has laid down her twigs the men come forward and place the larger branches they had gathered in an upright position inside the twigs. The guide lights the twigs and as the fire is burning one by one each person comes with that which symbolizes what they are letting go and expresses what they hope to receive, and giving their nature gift to the fire say something like: 'I give to the fire my insistence on always being right and I take from the fire humility in my heart.' When the large branches have been consumed by the fire, the guide leads the group in holding hands together, and chanting the following words they all move clockwise around the fire: 'We give thanks to the fire, for the passion of its burning. We give thanks to the fire, thanks and praise.' This little chant is repeated nine times and then the guide stands, releases her hands from the person at either side and brings the movement to a close. She then guides every-one into the *Seá*. Everyone then turns their backs to the dying embers and at the direction of the guide they all take three steps forward and disperse. The ritual is over and the rest of the evening's feasting can begin.

Bealtaine

Celebrated on 1 May, the word *Bealtaine* finds its origin in the Gaelic meaning the 'mouth of the fire'. Fire was a very important element in the lives of the Celts as it had the power of being destructive as well as creating heat and forging metals. It was also worshipped as a mighty purifier. It would also seem to hold within it the dark and the light. The bright flame of Brigit was seen to glow out of the dark and deep earth. May was a special time when Brigit was honoured for her care and attention of nature imbuing it with rich colours and abundant fruits. The 1 May celebrated the coming of summer, a time when the fairies or *sidhe* ('divas' or 'angels') came to dance joy and song into the earth, thus blessing all nature with their smiles from the sun. *Bealtaine* was also one of the great gods of life and death in as much as he had the power to create life and at the same time take it away.

It was a custom during the time of the Celts to light two fires on 1 May. Cattle were driven through the fires thus purifying them, and stirring the passion in them to give plenty of milk and produce good strong calves the following year. Young men danced through the fires also proving their courage and ensuring virility and strength. Naturally the young maidens watched on with a mixture of glee and ambivalence. It was also a practice for the young males to cut down branches from the hawthorn tree and place the flowers in the hair of a maiden they were attracted to, resulting in many new courtships. It was a time therefore when the passions of both animal and human alike were stirred up, and the earth celebrated her children with joy and Brigit and her beloved *Bealtaine* smiled on them and rejoiced.

It was on 1 May that a great and deadly pestilence befell the men of Parthalon, who had tried to conquer Ireland (name derived from the

Celtic goddess, *Eriu*), and most of his race was extinguished within a short time. The May-pole dance, which is still part of May Day celebrations in many parts of the British Isles, originated at this time. The pole represents the pestilence itself, whilst the colourful streamers flowing from the top symbolize the ways in which it spread from one to the other. The dance depicts the writhing of the bodies as they contracted the plague or petulance. So it was far from the gay and delightful merry-go-round of today.

In the month of May, we as young children loved the May procession, when a statue of the blessed Virgin Mary was carried around the village adorned with flowers and long veil. Young girls walked in front of the statue throwing rose petals and singing: 'Hail queen of heaven, *Ave Maria*, and hail queen of the May.' When we got home from the procession and we took off our 'first communion dresses' – white veil, good patent leather shoes, and white socks, and delighted in making a May altar in honour of the blessed Mother Mary. I remember gathering the wild flowers from the fields and putting them in jam jars on the altar. A statue of the Virgin Mother was adorned with primroses and daisies, and was placed on a white lace cloth in our bedrooms. Every night in the month of May we would kneel in front of the altar and say the rosary for 'purity of soul and body'. We also prayed for good health in mind and body for all members of the family, and especially for anyone in the parish who was unwell. This custom found its roots in Celtic times, when a young child would be honoured by the older maidens by being carried in a procession through the community, dressed in beautiful colours and draped in garlands of flowers. The young female child was called *cailín na mbláth* or 'flower girl'.

A ritual for *Bealtaine*

Following is a ritual for *Bealtaine*: Erect your own altar and place on it all the artifacts that are important to you. These could include a photograph of your family or friend or someone you do not see very often. Place a vase (or jam jar!) of flowers from your own garden or bought ones in the centre. Have a candle at either side and include nature gifts like shells, leaves, a stone, etc. If there is a special wish or prayer you have in your heart, write it down and put the piece of paper under the stone. Each morning and night read out loud your wish three times and then say the 'Seá' at the end. Do this for the 31 days in May and you may be delighted with the results! A friend did it last year and at the end of the month he met his now fiancé! Be sure you really want what you ask for!

Another suggestion for a ritual is the following: As May denotes the beginning of the summer solstice, it is good to welcome the sun into your life and give thanks for his warmth and vitality. At midday on May Day go into your garden and if the sun is visible look in his direction. With your arms stretched towards him, chant the words underneath and as you turn towards the four directions keep chanting (twelve times) as you move in the direction of north, south, east, and west.

> *I give thanks to the sun, for the life of my being,*
> *I give thanks to the sun, thanks and praise.*
> *I give thanks to the sun, for the wonders of creation,*
> *I give thanks to the sun, thanks and praise.*

Friends might like to celebrate with you so do invite them. It is usual in Celtic rituals to celebrate with food and a glass of wine or fruit juice after a ritual. Another way of celebrating the coming of summer is to participate in the 'stone prayers' or the 'wisdom of stones' ritual. The following is a guide: Gather nine small white stones. Write a number on each stone from one to nine. Put them in a bag. On white cards again write the numbers one to nine, and underneath each number write what it signifies, for example:

1. Union with all creation
2. Marriage of soul and spirit
3. Triple goddess/god
4. Crossroads
5. Magick
6. Courage
7. Worlds of the psyche
8. Healer

9.   Breath of the holy one

Prayers to match numbers

1.   May I learn, oh great breath,
     How to be at peace with all,
     That like me has made a home in the earth,
     May I learn the way of at-one-ment.

2.   Quicken your grace in me,
     That I may be able
     To surrender my will to yours,
     And to let go of my small mind.

3.   May Virgin, Mother, Crone,
     Youth, Father, Wise Man
     Dance in my bones
     And free my longing to belong.

4.   As I stand at the centre
     Of the crossroads,
     May I breathe in the clarity of your light
     And listen to your voice in me.

5.   May the magick of thy creation
     Delight my tired bones,
     And may all the worlds of beauty
     Make me more conscious.

6.   Grant me the courage
     To follow my soul's song.
     And when I stumble on the way,
     Bring me home to myself.

7. Let me not dwell in the house of ignorance,
   But lead me to the light,
   That I may see with the eyes of the moon
   And hear with patience.

8. Take my senses and make them pure,
   That I be a blessing to myself and others,
   And to all I encounter this day,
   And may healing flow in me.

9. Breathe in me,
   That my breath be a song to the earth,
   May I not hold on to what
   I think is mine,
   But let go into your love.

In a gathering of friends invite each one to shake the bag of stones three times in a circular movement, holding the top of the bag in their palm. Now ask them to put their hand in the bag and take out a stone. Let them go to the card with the appropriate number and read aloud what it says. They get to keep the stone and the card. Why not make up your own prayer stones and invite friends to join you. This is a very healing ritual to do at feasts like Christmas or Easter time, when friends are gathered together. I sometimes make little bags of stones and the accompanying cards, and give them as birthday gifts.

Lughnasa

Lughnasa is celebrated at the end of July, beginning August. The word *Lughnasa* comes from the god, *Lugh*, who was the son of the great sun god, *Kian*. *Lugh* was known as the lord of the light, although he spent most of his childhood in the underworld of darkness. Seemingly he understood the meaning of death and life, for he had experienced the land of the living, which was also called fairyland or land of the dead, and had returned to the land of humans bringing them light. In Celtic

Consciousness the underworld was not without the light, the mighty sun shone in both worlds, as he did not discriminate between the dimensions. This is an example to us to let our light shine indiscriminately, to have no judgements as to whom we should or should not love.

Lugh was the father of that great Irish mythological warrior *Cú Cuchulain* and it was said that he was guardian of the fort whilst his son slept. The work of the father to protect the son, to be his safe guard and to allow the son to sleep or to remain unconscious, whilst he, the father, stands guard over his soul, was natural to the order and ideology of the Celts. In contemporary language this could be translated as the father having healed his own dysfunctioning psychology could then be present for the son, not interfering in his life but providing him with a functioning role model. The idea of falling asleep for a certain length of time – three nights and three days, or three hundreds years – is not unusual in many of the myths and tales of the Celts. The time of so-called sleeping of course was symbolic also of travelling to the underworld of darkness and returning to this world with more wisdom, more integrated.

At *Lughnasa* we delight in celebrating the harvesting of our fruits as we enjoy the results of our labours. At this time of the year the men in the farming communities all gather together and help one farmer to 'take in the hay'. This is called the *meithéal*. It was and still is the women's job to brew the tea and bake the hot bread and bring it to the fields. Children happily joined in the day's work and in the evening all gathered again having washed and changed their clothes. The evenings gathering or *ceilidh* was always one of good storytelling and much merriment. Apples from the trees were eaten, and jams and marmalades were lavishly spread on the big fat oatmeal and soda bread scones.

The fiddle was usually brought down from the loft and a few good lively tunes would have brought the young and old on to the flag floors to dance the night away, or until the fiddler got thirsty. A cup of good strong tea and *uisge beatha* would have been his reward for having provided the music for the jigs and reels. In later times, dancing and merrymaking was frowned upon by most parish priests; and a *ceili* house was called 'the house of the devil himself'. I remember learning from the old ones that a certain priest not only disapproved of dancing, but put a curse on the ones who did!

The evil spell might have rendered the culprit immobile in the following way:

May the sun scorch the face of you,
May the wind take your feet to the sky,
May the rain pour rivers over you
And may you not eat fresh bread for a year and a day.

They used to say that if a priest put a spell on someone, their harvest would rot and their animals would all perish. Such was the power they possessed and some people were in dread of disobeying the 'good priest of God'.

As a child I loved to listen to the old ones telling the stories and reading the letters from their sons and daughters who had to go to Scotland and England for work. Usually one or two people in the parish were able to read and they had the prestigious job of reading the letters out loud for all to hear. Ahh! the humour and conviviality was soul food.

A ritual for *Lughnasa*

On the evening of 1 August prepare a basket of fruit, sweet breads, and vegetables, and lay it on the earth beside the place where a fire can be made. Gather some good friends and light a fire in the way proposed in the ritual for *Samhain* and *Imbolg*. When the fire is burning brightly, the guide asks those present to stand in a circle around the fire. Everyone holds their hands up in the air while they move three steps to the right, then three steps to the left. Now place the left foot over the right and then the right foot over the left and bring both feet together with a loud clap of their hands. You can add music to synchronize with the steps. Repeat this movement nine times. When this is finished, everyone sings the following little ditty as they dance around the fire (you can create your own musical accompaniment!):

We give thanks to the earth, for nourishing our lives.
We give thanks for the harvest safely brought home.
We give thanks for our friends and our families alike.
We give food to the people who have none.

The guide takes the basket of fruit and other goods, and from inside the circle she/he distributes the contents to all present, making sure there is still food left in the basket. (This will be later given to people, who do not have much food, or taken to hospitals and distributed to patients who do not have visitors.) Before the fire has gone out, everyone is invited to sit around it and tell stories. If someone does not have a story to tell they can dance or sing or recite poetry. The idea is that everyone gives from the harvest of their soul's creativity. Before the gathering disperses, the guide invites each one to name a dead relative and a prayer such as the following is said out loud by the guide:

With plenty in our bellies, and the fire in our heart,
We send you greetings from the meithéal ('gathering') tonight,
May the dark of the earth sustain you with ease,
May the joy of the sun shine you his light.

Meditative celtic blessings
– blessing branches

To create a blessing branch for yourself, you need to first gather all the following materials: pieces of ribbon, coloured cords, wool, feathers, beads, old earrings, necklaces, bits of straw, chamois cloth, sequins, and such like (coloured materials to include black). Place all on your table. You will also need: a pair of scissors, needle and thread, and strong adhesive. As nature herself is a rich source of blessing we add to this by consciously including her creation in our prayers and blessing for ourselves and others. Branches and twigs, stones and feathers, animal skins and hair, pebbles, seeds, shells, etc., are invaluable materials, which I use in the making of blessing branches. The following is one of the many ways they may be used. Consciously go into nature and pick a bare branch about 45cm long, and about 2.5cm in diameter. Give thanks for the branch and consider the journey this little branch had to make to get to you, from seedling to tree, from tree to branch, and from connection with the tree to its fallen place on the earth. Consider what might have been the rest of its journey had you not noticed it, and picked it up. Bring the branch to your table.

Now light a candle and do the following meditation/visualization. What is the deepest and greatest gift you could bring to yourself in this moment? As you hold the naked branch in your hands imagine that you feel and see the gift coming towards you. Notice how you are feeling and with these feelings begin to colour the branch with a piece of material.

Keep visualizing and with the feelings associated with this wonderful gift coming towards you continue to adorn the branch. This may be with beads or feathers or whatever colours symbolically represent your gift. When you get to the top of your branch cut a small square of material and put a special bead or gem inside it representing your gift and blessing. Then with a piece of gold thread, or any colour you choose, tie it round the material to make a small bag. Tie it to the branch. Please remember if the gift you have asked for is to your soul's advantage you will certainly experience it. If not then you will receive another gift just as wonderful (sometimes we do not know what we ask for).

At the top of the branch it is a good idea to tie a feather thus symbolizing freedom and lightness. May you always be free to choose consciously so that the consequences may be joy filled. When you have finished making your blessing branch stay in silence for a while holding the beautifully adorned branch close to your heart. Breathe in the love and good energy you put into making it and give thanks for the practice.

I love to make blessing branches with friends. It is such a lovely way to enjoy being creative together. Blessing branches may be made for friend's birthdays, weddings or anniversaries, or as a gift for any occasion. They may be made as gifts for children and young people going on journeys. They carry good vibrations and are a source of great comfort to many who are far from family. It is a lovely gift to teach children. On a rainy day they love nothing better than to sit with mum or dad, or their little friends and make as a four year old called her 'bressing branches'.

Children understand the deeper meanings involved and one child only five years old made one for her mother who was undergoing an operation. She and her dad came to the hospital and presented mum with a beautifully coloured branch, which was a great delight and joy to the mother. Children in hospitals love to make them and give them as gifts to the nurses and doctors and their carers. One child who was dying made one for her aunt whom she hadn't seen for a long time, and left a message 'This is for my aunt because I will not see her again, but it is full of music and dance, and song, and love, and hugs.' When the aunt received it with the messages she was truly delighted. Schools should add this exercise to their schedules. It helps the child's creative powers. It also helps their dexterity, and it would be a way of keeping one of the old rituals alive.

There are many other blessing branches one could make, for example, *a life branch*, which entails a blessing received in the remembering of one's whole life. It is as follows: Set your table as above. This time have a pencil and paper to hand and make sure you have gold-coloured thread. With the same mindfulness as before, find two branches the same length; bring them to your table and cross them over. Light your candle. Whatever your age is now divide it by four. If, for example, you are 55 years old, that gives each of the four quadrants 13 and three quarters. Each of the four will represent different stages/ages going clockwise from birth to 13 years, from 14 to 27 years, from 28 to 41 years, and from 42 to 55 years. If you are 43 years old that gives you 10 and three quarters in each quadrant so you will arrange your years thus: from birth to 10 years, from 11 to 21 years, from 22 to 32 years, and from 33 to 43. Having made out your own chart, close your eyes and visualize your life.

Go back to the day you were conceived. How were you feeling about coming to earth? Go to the day you were born. Can you imagine what that experience was like for you? Now go through your life as dictated by your age chart. Lovingly, go through each year's section and feel into the years, expressing whatever comes along. (Oftentimes it feels so good to have your life branch witnessed by others. It gives a feeling of comfort and togetherness.) When you have done this stay in silence for another while. As you give thanks for having come to earth and for living as consciously as you can then begin to make your life branch as follows.

Tie the two branches together with a gold-coloured thread, forming a shape like an x. The gold symbolizes the gold centre of your own being, your own divine nature. Begin at the centre and with mindfulness of your first quarter years, work with your coloured materials from the centre to the end of the branch. (As you finish each quarter branch place a feather at the top.) Whatever you feel allow it to be felt in you.

Take your time. You have plenty of it. Now go to the next section of years, and from the centre again work to the end of the next branch with coloured materials, beads etc. (always working clockwise), until you have completed your life branch. Now you will see the colourful way in which you have lived through your visualization of your life to this day.

The old way was for a very old person to make their life branch and it was then put on their chest when they died. It was either burned or placed in the earth with them. Like the symbology of the empty bowl, as described before, or feeding back the story, the life branch was taken by the ancestors and they blessed the soul as it travelled to its resting place with no unfinished earth business. I do not want to be nearing body death before I appreciate my wondrous life, so every so many years I make a life branch… like making a will, updating it every so often.

There are very many ways to enrich ourselves with the making of blessing branches. May you enjoy the ones I shared with you, and like many others do please let me know how you are enjoying doing them either alone, with children, or in groups.

Chapter 10

Cycles of Day and Night

Daytime cycle

The idea that every new day is a blessing and another chance to be in life lies very deep in the Celtic consciousness. To awaken each day with a sense of gratitude in one's heart that we still have another day in which to live our lives fully is a direct teaching from Celtic Consciousness. The following prayer is an example:

I awaken this day to the Grace of love's blessing.
I awaken this day to the sound of love's song.
I awaken this day to the wind of love's challenge.
I awaken this day to the joy in my bones.

This is a translation of a Gaelic chant I learned approximately half a century ago in a little old stone school in Donegal. We spoke only Gaelic, and this tune has stayed with me all those years. For me words like love, grace, sound, wind, joy, blessing, song, challenge, and bones weave themselves around these images of awakening. This awareness of the blessings in our lives, and gratitude for all of life's graces is the essence of Celtic Consciousness. We have a saying in Donegal 'How are you gathering yourself into the day?' It is about gathering ourselves, about herding ourselves in, like the gathering of the hay in the summer, and the herding in of the cows. It is the gathering of our own harvest. With a grateful heart we gather all our experiences of our dreams and night visions, and gather them into the open heart ready for a new day.

Grateful heart

In 2004 I attended a family constellations workshop in Germany and found it strange when the therapist admonished me for having said 'thank you' when it was my turn to take part in a 'constellation'. He maintained that my gratitude was a dysfunction adding that I must have little self-esteem otherwise I could accept without saying thank you. This dear man was seemingly unable to grasp the richer meaning of openness to receiving, and the fact that it had nothing to do with feelings of inferiority. Being grateful for all the gifts in life and being open to taking in leaves us richer.

Hospitality and the caring of neighbours are innate in the Celtic psyche. An Irish saying: *faoi scáth a chéile a mhaireann na daoine* means 'it is under the shadow of each other that we live'. Ireland is known as 'the island of the many welcomes' and when I go abroad I am never surprised to hear of our people being spoken of as being very friendly and open to the stranger. The old ones would have said that 'There's no one that you could be calling a stranger, now is there? Sure, aren't we all the one way made and the one way needing?'

I remember as a child living with my Nanny during the school holidays in a place called Kilraine, a beautiful rural countryside in Donegal, full of standing stones, which were called 'grandmothers', and open expanse of green meadows and mountains that smiled down on the small rivers and thatched cottages. Nanny never closed the door at night or ever turned away a stranger who came to the door. The kettle was always 'on the boil' and the black cauldron was always on the crook of the open fire, boiling the stew. It certainly represented Bronwen's Cauldron of abundance! The stew consisted of good big potatoes, a leg of mutton, all kinds of vegetables, oatmeal dumplings, crubeens (pig trotters), carrageen moss (a very nutritious seaweed), and Guinness stout. Whoever came to visit was told to sit down and a mug of the 'stuff from the pot' was given to them. If someone looked a bit 'under the weather' (not feeling very well), they got a jam jar of *uisge beatha* ('whiskey') to wash it down well! One old man remarked: 'There's eating and drinking in Nanny McDyre's stew!'

Nanny would always give some to the dog under the table and leave some for the 'wee folks' or fairies at night. Many were the *scéalta* ('stories'), that were told and naturally added to, of how the fairies in Kilraine were the first to ever dance an Irish jig, and this was after they had consumed her magick potion! Somehow she always included the animals and the fairies in most of her rituals; and night prayers or *beannachtaighe na h-oiche* were never complete without mention of them. It was such a wonderful feeling of security for me as a young child to hear Nanny praying as I lay in the small hand-made bed in the alcove near the fire, the soft down of duck wrapped around me, listening to her droning, whilst the ticking from the old grandfather clock reassured our existence in time, and the dark drapes of night hushed the day to rest. For these gifts I am truly grateful.

Nanny's hospitality extended to children who also received from her in the form of a sweet from the long pocket of her big black apron, which she never took off. In it she kept a never-ending supply of hard-boiled sweets called 'brandy balls'. They were hard black and white striped sweets without paper that were sold in large glass jars, and could be bought two ounces at a time. She always kept one of these sweets in the bottom of her pocket, and it was usually covered in dog's hairs and bits of soil. When the children came to visit her, she would stand them all beside the table and ritualistically say:

> '*I wonder if the fairies have left a sweet for us today?*'

The children always smiled because they knew they would not be disappointed. Still they would wait in happy anticipation. Down into the long pocket Nanny would guide her right hand, and as if curiously exploring the depths of treasury itself she would grunt:

> '*I wonder what we have here now.*'
> '*A sweet, a sweet*' the children would answer in chorus.
> '*Ahh! but what kind of sweet?*'
> '*A brandy ball, a brandy ball.*'

Up came the hand with the brandy ball. Without another word, she would put the sweet in her own mouth, and suck the hairs off it, spit them out, and then put it into the mouth of the first child waiting in line. The others would wait patiently for their 'turn' to suck it. Having gone round the children, the sweet now in diminished form came back to Nanny for the final crunch of it between the few back teeth left. The children got what they came for every time, and Nanny was always there to provide it. She never engaged in any other conversation with them, it was as if the words spoken between her and the young people became sacred and part of the ritual. I loved Nanny's brandy balls and so did the other children. I could not imagine this happening nowadays! Parents would have her arrested for unhygienic practices at least! But in those days somehow, it was seen as an act of love. I told this story at one of my gatherings in France with German people.

They really enjoyed it until at the end of the session I put my hand into my long pocket and said 'Now I have a present from my grand-mother.' The group, transfixed, went into shock. Immediately taken from their place of comfort to a place of fear – would we have to suck a brandy ball? When I took out a banana and began to peel it, relief was shown on their faces. As each person bit off some of the banana, love and gratitude soared to my grandmother on the wings of delighted German faces. Somehow, their own ancestors became part of the ritual too. Some-how, everyone present was taken into the energy of the grandmother where they became the child partaking in the ritual.

From mid-summer's day (21 June), when the weather was warm, a huge peat fire was lit every day outside. The big black cauldron was filled with potatoes, placed on the crook attached to a black crane that was forged to the stone wall behind, and lowered into the fire. When the 'spuds' (pota-toes) were boiled, 'scallions' (spring onions) and salt were added and with the words 'In the name of the Father and of the son and of the Holy Ghost.' the whole lot was mashed together. This was called 'poundies', which were heaped on to each plate by Nanny with a ladle. Everyone made a well in the centre into which they put a large clump of home made salty butter that had been churned that morning. Everyone sat happily around the fire with a big mug of fresh buttermilk to wash it all down. It was said that a man could go to work in the fields after his dinner (dinner was at 1.00 p.m. in those days) and not feel hungry until 7.00 p.m.!

In many places in the summer in Donegal there were special poundies for the men only, 100 percent proof homemade liquor called 'poteen' or 'mountain dew' was poured into the well in the centre instead of butter! This drink was said to give a man the power to lift a cart and horse and not bother him! It was also said that after a mug full of the stuff a man could drone the 172 verses of the *Beati*, which was an ancient Celtic psalm, without taking a breath! These times have died out, the fires are not lit outside so much, the psalm of Colmkille is no longer recited, and the mountain dew is no longer brewed up in the mountains! But some good rituals do not die out. We still invite the stranger into our homes in Donegal, as we are 'all in the one way of needing'.

A ritual for daytime

When you open your eyes to the morning, it is a good idea to lie in bed for a few minutes, and if you remember a dream to write it down. There may be a message that you need to hear from it. If your body/mind is without pain and you feel fine, just stop, take a deep breath and give thanks to the cosmos, or to god/goddess or to your own wise self that you are well and fit to meet the day. If you are in bed and not feeling good, lie quietly for a few seconds and inwardly look at your body/mind and talk to it lovingly like you would to a child who is ill. This is the time to give great and loving compassion to yourself. If you are in hospital and not feeling good, take time before your doctor does his rounds to have that inner dialogue or inner comforting of yourself. It will serve you well to hear your own voice mercifully acknowledging you at the beginning of the day.

You could speak to yourself and say: 'I know you are not feeling so well today; I just want you to know that I love you deeply, and I really care for you. What do you need right now? I will not leave you this day. I am close to your heart, and I am sorry you are not feeling so good.' I also suggest that you embrace your painful self lovingly in the way that is right for you, in the way you maybe longed to be held as a child or young person. It is not too late to be a good mother and father to yourself. You may think it strange to talk to yourself thus, but I know this small exercise has been a great help to people who live alone or are in hospital.

We need to hear the sound of our own voice reassuring us that we are alright. It is the voice of love and we are love. Indeed I have often spoken to myself in times of stress and worry, as at such times we often revert to the small child who cannot think what to do as the child only knows how to feel her world, and naturally cannot access adult reason. Therefore I will tell myself to 'Slow down, that's it, good! Now, take a deep breath, good now another.' This type of inner dialogue helps us to be more conscious in our dealings with the world, and ensures that we take care of ourselves in times of stress when we cannot 'think straight'.

During your day it is helpful to notice the blessings as they come your way. Be grateful for them out loud as this verifies their existence, and opens your heart up even more to the fullness of your day. I often thank the trees for looking so totally majestic, and the birds for singing me a morning song. I also talk to cows in the fields, and thank them for showing me how to slow down and take my time! Daisies and sunsets also delight my heart so much that I cannot be quiet in my pleasure. I am sure people have wondered who my invisible friends were at times when I have quite audibly appraised, 'Thank you, dear wind, I really need you in my head to clear my thoughts!' The Celtic Christians believed in the grace of 'gifting' one another with heart gifts; the idea being that as we gifted another, the gift is also ours, as we only receive in life from the abundance already pouring from the fountain of blessing.

Offering of gifts

There is a very loving way to offer a 'heart gift' to another, and it is as follows:

- Press your thumbs together and with your left hand cradling your right hand, bring them to your chest.
- Bowing towards the other whilst directing the cradled hands towards them say: 'From my heart to your heart.'
- Raising both hands to the sky continue: 'I bring you the gift of joy.'
- Bowing again to your friend with open hands say: 'That you be blessed in receiving.'
- Returning hands to one's own heart again say: 'That I be blessed in receiving.'

Brigit teaches that when we are grateful for a gift bestowed on us by another it is important that our thanks be triple thus the 'triple thanks' which is described in the following.

Ritual of thanksgiving

Thank you, thank you, thank you. The first thanks is to the person bringing the gift. The second thanks is to the gift itself, and the third thanks is to me for being open to receive. One does not have to repeat the thanks out loud, once suffices, but don't forget to quietly repeat it two more times in your heart. By doing the 'triple thanks' you are disposing yourself to receiving further from the universe.

Being aware of how you interact with others is very 'conscious making'. The people who annoy you who do not seemingly bring you blessing may be there to show you something about you! The ones that delight your heart are the more obvious blessing bringers. They also show you something about you. No matter whom you encounter, you will always be meeting up with yourself in different disguises! And that is exciting and wonderful. When we see all as gifts, we will live in peace and gratitude for everything we encounter. I have a long way to go yet because I certainly have not reached the place where I see everything as a gift the moment it is presented to me. It takes some distancing from it to really see the teaching and the healing in some situations in my life. I must be a slow learner!

Night-time cycle

Letting go of the day's activities with a reminder of all the blessings it held was an important ritual for the Celts. Night-time was the time when the spirit of darkness came to close the day in sleep. This she did more gradually during the summer cycle than the winter cycle. Awareness of death was natural to the Celtic psyche and night-time was said to be the most popular time when death came to take a soul to the 'summerlands' or as already referred to *tír na-n-óg*. It was also the time when *Dubha,* the goddess of the dark, came to invite bodied souls to go to the underworld and watch with the souls who had died, and were still suffering, as they could not get to the summerlands or *tír na-n-óg* themselves. These in-bodied souls were called watchers.

Today it is one of my practices as a priestess of Brigit to do 'Watching with the dying', which includes going into the underworld and following the soul's journey of *aite* or 'passages', or in Tibetan philosophy, *bardos,* to the place of peace and rest. This ritual takes place during the time the person is dying, and for three days afterwards. (see *A Celtic Book of Dying*[xiii])

I have a distinct memory of the *night-time rituals* that took place in our house as a young child. Angelus time, 6.00 p.m., was 'time for tea', after which preparation for nightfall took place. In most Catholic homes the rosary was said to honour Mary, mother of Jesus, and all members of the family had to be present for this. It wasn't the praying of the prayers of the rosary that tired us children, but the so-called 'trimmings'.

By the time all the prayers were said and a few amens were grunted back it was time for bed. Though the saying of the rosary took much longer than intended in the beginning, it was a way of acknowledging the need to be conscious of letting go of the day and remembering the final letting go of death. The readiness to die, and again, the idea of letting go of the day's problems, giving thanks for all that the day brought, is a recurring factor in the Celtic cycles of life in general, and one that the Christian Church continued through the ages. Close connection with the worlds of spirit was not foreign to me.

A ritual for night-time

When you are going to bed at whatever time, preferably before midnight (after midnight we are then into another day's energy), slow everything down. Do not eat after 7.00 p.m. because this disturbs the digestive tract cycle and could prevent sleep. A reliable way of slowing down the breath is as follows (if you have low blood pressure, be careful):

—   Either sit on your chair or wait until you are in bed and slowly breathe in, noticing the belly expanding as you do so. Slowly breathe out to exhale all the breath. Do this five times.

—   When you have breathed out, wait for the count of two before breathing in again. Having breathed in again, hold for the count of two. Keep these rhythms going for the next five breaths.

—   After a while you do not have to concentrate on the counting, just let the breath come slowly and go slowly. You will have established a gentle orderly rhythm, which will help you relax.

I always advise people when they are in bed at night to imagine their angel, or guide, or loving spiritual companion sitting at the bottom of the bed keeping watch over them as they sleep, especially if they cannot fall asleep easily or are feeling anxious. Indeed, I have suggested to some people to place a symbol of their loving guide on a chair beside the bed, and to be reassured that they are guided into sleep.

Chapter 11

Transitions

Helping the dying

A woman said she wanted to assist me with the dying. Having given me her phone number, I decided to call on her help with a young mother who was dying of cancer. The telephone conversation went as follows:

> *'Mary, I need some help with Mrs. Smith and her family, and you did say you would be available to help.'*
> *'Yes, Phyllida, I will drop everything. Tell me where you are, and I will go today.'*
> *'Mary, the help I need is as follows. Can you please collect her two children from school? When you get to the house, maybe you could help to clean up the kitchen.'*
> *'But Phyllida, I said I wanted to be with the dying.'*
> *'Yes, I know, and right now this work needs to be done.'*
> *'Phyllida dear, you know I have arthritis, and it is difficult for me to do heavy work.'*
> *'Thank you Mary, but please remember you can also serve the dying by collecting their children from school, and cleaning their kitchens.'*

Somehow, people have the idea that working with the dying at home means that they sit at the bedside and either pray for them, or insist on holding their hand, (their own fear) and every five minutes ask if they need something. At other times, helpers can be of great benefit to the dying by being the dying person's advocate.

I have a story about this too. My dear friend, Jo, was dying in hospital in Northern Ireland üand had advised me that she did not want to see the parish priest, while he was doing his rounds of the 'Catholics' in the ward. Reassuring her that I would do my best to keep him out, she continued reading her love story. The priest, having seen her Catholic name on the door, (that's another story!), knocked once, and opened the door. I immediately grabbed the magazine; Jo closed her eyes and pretended to be asleep. I went towards the door before the priest could enter, and advised him that she did not want to be disturbed.

'She will be more disturbed,' said he, 'if she realizes that I have been and gone, and she did not get the last rites. You may not know it Mrs Templeton (my married name) that Catholics have to have the last rites before they die.'

'I am aware of those facts,' I answered, 'but Jo has assured me that she has no sins she needs absolved.'

'Tell her when she wakens, that I will be back tomorrow, and I will see her then.'

At this stage I wondered what I should do, and so I told the priest that I would phone him later that evening, and talk about Jo's situation. When I came back into the room, she sat up in bed, smiling from ear to ear, and said 'Thank God I did not have to pretend to have sins. I am alright with God, Phyllida. I can go anytime, but I don't want to see that man again.' That evening, I called the priest and explained to him, in as compassionate a way as I could, that Jo did not want to have the priest when she was dying. I was lectured on the Catholic way of death, and I am sure the poor man was very surprised when I ended my conversation with the following 'I am sorry that this causes you grief, and I do know about the Catholic Church. I was a nun for four years. We have to listen to the needs of the dying, whether we believe in those needs or not.'

What would you bring to the dying? My friend, how are you with the living? How do you deal with relationships in your everyday life, with the so-called living? How congruent are you within yourself? Please remember you bring all of this to the dying.

- Bring the dying the gift of your own life, fully lived in every moment.
- Bring them your broken heart, in pain and grief.
- Bring them your joy, your dreams well dreamt.
- Bring them your experiences of your passion for life.
- Bring them your willingness to die many times every day, and go beyond surviving.
- Bring them your tears, if tears there be.
- And if the sun is shining, smile it to them,
- Then open the window and let them fly.

Having trained with Elisabeth Kübler-Ross, and having worked subsequently with many people living and dying, I realize the importance of maintaining a grounded, natural, open, vulnerable space within myself, at all times. There is no difference for me between befriending the living, and so-called dying. Why should I change my personality to fit in with the pseudo image of death? If I wear colourful clothes, have a red streak in my hair, why would I suddenly change my appearance, to a more sombre one and, therefore, change my attitude to the dying? Being authentic is all important in all our relationships. Saying no to a dying person can be an act of love; just as saying no to a person fully in life can. There is a story…

Tough love

My friend's mother was dying at home, and she asked me to visit. I was happy to say yes. When I arrived at the house, I realized my friend was totally exhausted trying to fulfill every wish her mother expressed. I asked my friend why she was burning out, and not asking for help.

'My mother will only have me with her.' she replied, through darkened eyes.

'This is not serving you or your mother.' I replied. When I realized that the latter insisted on my friend sitting with her, hour after hour, in case she would need something, I advised that neighbours could provide the same works of mercy, and give my friend a break.

'Well you tell her, not me.' was my friend's retort.

We spoke a long time that night, alone, despite her mother's insistence that we speak in her presence, in her room. Eventually, my friend understood about tough love, and simply told the facts to her mother and said that the neighbours would come and be with her, and give my friend a break. At first her mother was indignant, and said 'No, I don't want them to come.' but when I reasoned with her, that her daughter would become ill, she finally gave in. This woman did not die for another six weeks, and thankfully, my friend was able to have a good break, and be energized herself. Love is no less love that says no, either to the living or the dying.

The timing of things

Seemingly in Celtic times as people were ageing and unable to live satisfying lives within the family and community they would sit down with their family and ask them questions regarding how they had been as parents, how wise had they been in the guiding of grandchildren, and asked each member what gifts they had given them. They then shared with the family that their time in earth plane had come to an end, and named the time when they would leave it. When that day came they administered poisoned berries to each other, and died together. Seemingly, this was known as *marbh trathúil* – 'timed death'. This was not an everyday ritual; only elderly parents who felt they wanted to leave the earth whilst still in sound mind did so. One wonders what their fears of frailty were and if they felt they would be a burden to the family. Nowadays the same problems arise in the psyches of our older folks and there is a divided debate on the issue of voluntary euthanasia. As already stated any choice taken out of fear is in fact not a true choice.

The theology, psychology, and sociology around conscious dying expands our awareness into asking new questions, providing new information, and seeking open discussion with regard to death, the family and God. Therefore, we are also being led into a more creative experience of the dying process. Does conscious dying suggest that one has the right to decide where, when, and how one dies? The answer to the first of these questions would seem to be the one that receives more attention – I want to die at home in my own bed, friends around, funeral planned, will written, place of burial arranged – all the physical, homely, and practical preparations done. It scares us when we look at the when and how of our dying. Immediately, morals, God, religion, and societal values present difficulties. Are these difficulties culturally defined, religiously defined, or socially and theologically so ingrained as to prevent any personal and subjective movement?

Whether it is known universally or not, many medical people do intervene when death is imminent. Much 'terminal sedation' or pain relief is acceptable as it is all about keeping a patient comfortable, keeping the body so-called alive, and without pain. The medicine is given with full knowledge that it will suppress the respiratory system making each breath shallower. In other words this hastens the death of the patient. This is not called euthanasia as we know it, but is a medically acceptable way of helping with 'happy death'. So do we have a right to intervene in the when and how of our own death? Does conscious dying suggest just that – that we consciously decide when our life should end? But surely that is to suggest that should life prove too difficult we just commit suicide. If there were no religion, no God to answer to, no societal laws and regulations would we in fact 'take our lives in our own hands'?

It is somehow totally unethical, absolutely against God's laws, and leaves a sense of disgust within the psyche of conscious human beings when a young man on death row is taken, blindfolded, in fear, and put into an electric chair, leaving his family grieving. He is then willfully, and with the blessing of God given by a pastor, killed with a gallery full of witnesses (an eye for an eye sanctioned by religion and the state). Picture, at the same time an old woman, lying in a hospital bed, conscious, crying, asking, and pleading with the doctor 'I am 87 years of age, I am at peace with my god, I have lived a good life.

I don't want to see my children having to come distances every day to see me. I don't want to go on and on like this, where there is no dignity. Please give me an injection to end it all.' And the doctor keeping the rules and regulations of his Hippocratic Oath, and societal and religious values has to deny this. When her pain gets worse or a chest infection sets in, and she is no longer conscious then he may order terminal sedation.

Please consider these two situations; I cite them for us to consider not as a means of doling out blame or reaching ultimatums. In both situations it seems that medication is being used as punishment. In the case of the man in the electric chair this is evident whilst the old woman experiences suffering in the withholding of medication. She may also perceive this as punishment.

Other ways of unconsciously hastening death in some homes for the elderly are:

1. Inappropriate food for the requirements of the patient.
2. Withholding assistance during meal-times, due to lack of staff and general care.
3. Putting meals out of reach of patients, for instance, on a tray at the bottom of the bed.
4. Failure to provide prescribed supplementary foods.
5. Poor oral hygiene.
6. Failure to meet elimination needs.
7. Infrequent mobilization.
8. Failure to meet cultural needs.
9. Inadequate pain relief.

You may doubt that this happens but malnutrition is common in elderly patients in prolonged care.

At the age of 82, my father was admitted to hospital because of heart failure. Against his own will he was fed naso-gastrically, which made him sick and created distress. We as a family demanded that his request i.be. not to be fed be granted even though we knew that it would hasten his death. When we took him home however, we were able to fulfill his every need. On one occasion in hospital I personally removed the tubes so that my father could breathe properly and not feel the distension in his stomach. When my mother was dying in hospital she pulled out the tubes herself and was admonished like a bold child for having done so. For many people the thought of not being able to control their dying process leaves them with a sense of helplessness, and with no sense of inner authority.

How can it be that a person of sound mind through life and of ample consciousness during dying is often treated like a child in so far as the state, authority, and religion take over? Surely, dignity is something not only reserved for the living, but must be afforded the dying, and dignity for many people includes choosing consciously when they deem it is time for them to leave their bodies. This is a debate that must again offer as much information as possible. Maybe it is time to look upon a 'happy death' as the soul prerogative of the dying person having made a living will, and testifying how they should die.

My personal belief is that we will learn lessons up until our last breath, and although my 'living will' suggests that I do not want to be resuscitated, nor fed when I reach my last days, I still want drops of water administered orally. Living consciously in the meantime, and working on my unfinished business (dying every day) will leave me clear to leave behind the physical and move into the fantastic adventure of dying when the natural time for this comes. If we had more education about the dying process maybe people would feel more inner authority regarding their dying process. They would be in more contact with their soul's inner timing and be aware of the physical shifts of energy. As I endeavour to live more and more soulfully whilst in a body, I know that when death comes, I will greet it with the same sense of wonder as I do my bodied life. This said, I still am very aware of the need to challenge the status quo regarding choosing the time of death. Keeping an open heart to all situations helps me to listen with mercy.

Feeding back the story

It was an old Celtic custom that either a neighbour or a good friend sat with the ill person while they were still incommunicado, and scribed their story as was told to them by the dying person. The friend then fed them back the story to them, emphasizing the various incidents, and important experiences of their lives. Often photographs accompanied the event, and the dying person was able to discuss and re-experience each event. The idea behind this was that the dying person could absorb their own story in their bodies so that when they died the soul energy brought the story forward into their new life. Beings in this new life were made aware of the life journey of this newly arrived soul, and congratulated them for having finished the course.

Clay was also used as a container of the story, whereby the ill person, while telling their own story to a friend, moulded and kneaded the clay on a tray on the bed, thus earthing the story so they could then leave it behind, with no unfinished business. The friend, then holding the clay towards the ill person, recounted their story. It was important that the full story be told without judgement or criticism, and that every so-called mistake could be forgiven, before the dying person left their clay body behind. Often the friend or watcher would surrogate absent people the dying person wanted to speak with. If forgiveness was needed then this was possible.

Dancing was also used as a container for the story, whereby, a young dancer was brought in, listened to the story, and then intuitively, danced back her/his dance of living and dying, so that the ill person could feel the movement in their own body, and then let go of it. It was about remembering movement, remembering their dance of life, and, going further and deeper into that dance, into the dance of dying.

Many times in Ireland, the life was sung back to the person with spontaneous music coming from the soul of the singer. The musical content was akin to Indian folk music; here again, the influence of the East in our Irish traditional music. Music, it was said, went deeper into the psyche than words, to touch the soul's own musical note with which it was seduced to earth, and to clear the pathway for the soul's note.

Death mourning was the name given to death music, which in the Gaelic was called *seisig-bhais*. This music was in the form of a lament or dirge, and usually sung by an older woman or crone. It started off as a howl from the womb, reaching a crescendo with a loud screech. The name of the dead person was sung over, and over again, like a mantra usually ending with the words *oconoconooh*, which translated means 'oh sorrow, oh sorrow'. This lament was then taken up by those present in the room, as if in answer to the crone's cry. I remember, as a child, joining in thinking it was like the sound of the sea, like the sound of the *bean sidhe*. No doubt after the lament was over, singing and dancing took over.

Nowadays, people attend schools of thanantology to learn Gregorian music accompanied by the harp to assist the dying. Therese Shroeder-Sheker had a school in America for such training. She believes that the dying are better assisted to leave their earth bodies whilst listening to unfamiliar music played on a harp and sung. The musicians sit at either side of the bed, and sing in the higher octaves to attract the soul out of the body.

The Celtic way, the way of our ancestors, is to be with the natural, the known, and the hearth, to be with the sound of our neighbours natural rhythmic tones – clay tones, earth tones; to be with the barking of the dogs, and the smell of the soup from the kitchen, to be with the sound of the fiddler in the parlour, and the sound of the cows in the field behind the bedroom. My friend Hannah wants to hear the sound of the donkeys braying, carrying her on the breath of their sounds. The comfort of the 'known' for many dying people is beyond measure. The Celtic soul is very comfortable with nature, the natural, the known, with the every-day, which naturally transcends the ordinary to include mystery, transformation, and death. Aye.

My work is to bring death out of the parlour, out of the 'good room', the tidy, well-dusted room where we wear our good clothes, where we don't speak out of turn, where everything is nice and neat. Birth is not tidy. Living is not tidy so why should we try to domesticate death? The open heart of death that I referred to in my previous book invites all of us, our untidy, as well as tidy, our competent as well as vulnerable, our knowing, and our unknowing to sit at its table, and eat from the foods that have been well baked in the oven of wisdom. Then the fat bread of living can nurture us at a deeper level, as we live the paradoxes of mystery, of my story and your story, living and dying. So many people have prayed for 'happy deaths', to die properly, to die with a smile on their face, whilst in body form have sought happiness only through success in the acquisition of material things. My friend Ian Oughtred's mother, Jean Oughtred, wrote the following before she died: 'I have been imprisoned by ideologies and dogma. I had been liberated into the recognition that all manifestations of life are precious for their own sake, and so am I. Respect for self is part of interacting with other lives, other beings, all the processes of life itself comprising a whole. Isn't life full of miraculous forms of being, always changing in form, constantly renewing, never ending. I just feel so sorry for those immersed in battles for things, fashions, successes; all very nice, but never satisfying.'

The physical body and the psyche

By observing the body and its structure/skeletal form, one can easily determine the emotional status operating behind that appearance. This is known as body symbology or body geography. From the emotional status the state of the psyche can be determined. This may seem like an arrogant assumption. However, is it not feasible to suggest that a certain bodily frame can easily determine the general state of the carrier of that frame? It would seem logical that the body expresses the status of soul energy. If the soul has a certain agenda, and the personality is unaware of such, and is on a more egotistical route, this will be manifested in the body.

The work of the soul is to awaken the personality. The Celtic expression is *gutha* – 'to call back' or 'to remind', or *airscroí*, which means literally 'to reheart': to place in the heart that which we had forgotten. In these days where dear souls would seem to experience great pain in decision making; great trauma in personal relationships; great suffering because of attachments; and general discontent about political situations I believe we must develop and build up a strong spiritual immune system. How might we do this? You will have your ways, and I support you totally in this. I suggest cultivating self-compassion, walking our spiritual talk, conscious involvement with the world, showing kindness to all beings, dealing with whatever emotional upsets present themselves in that moment

When we practise these disciplines our dysfunctioning emotions are transformed, and in the transformation love can breathe, but practise makes perfect! I find I can do most of the above for a whole day, and maybe half of the next day, but certainly by the third day I am back to square one. Sometimes I give the excuse to myself in the following ways: I am too tired. I can't be bothered. What does it matter? Nothing helps. I am deluding myself. After all these excuses I realize it is my earth-mind keeping me with the status quo, reinforcing old habits, and afraid to step into the world of change. The demands of a popular culture – to succeed, to achieve, to win, to get to the so-called top, to stay alive and youthful looking at all costs even if this should entail cosmetic surgery to delay the ageing process or to have heart and organ transplants to defy death – cause much disturbance to the psyche.

Organ/blood donation

It is interesting to know that in the time of the Celts, when a person became ill, herbs and healing plants were administered to them, also water from mountain streams to which they added their own blessings. When an internal organ was dysfunctional they made a replica out of wood or stone and buried it in the earth with an incantation to the Great Mother to promote healing. When headache or insanity were the problem, a hole was bored through the head to release the spirit of darkness that was said to possess the patient. Any illness that could not be healed by means of surgery, herbs and plants, or the application of damp clay (which was applied to aches and pains), was seen as possession of a dark spirit, or because of their own dark deeds.

The wise ones were then able to perform rituals of dispossession. Older women, the crone, were said to possess healing qualities given in gratitude from the earth – *mar gheal ar an fodladh dearg a thainig ó bhroin an chailín*. This means 'because of the red blood that was given from the womb of the young woman'. This healing took the form of *beannaíonn* or a 'cradle blessing' with soothing sounds. Many people are moved to donate parts of their bodies when they die. This is such a commendable act of love, which according to Buddhism will gain merit for that soul.

In our tradition however, we believe that we come to earth each time with a distinct body through which the soul will manifest herself. As we are systems of energy, we have to wonder about the full impact of taking on another's organ. If we believe that each cell in the body has a memory, has its own source of intellectual acumen that holds information for that individual alone then all the experiences of one's life accumulates in that individual's own databank. Although surgeons make sure that the right tissue match is made, nevertheless the recipient does not always accept the donor organ. Is this the body's own wisdom, and is it ethical to insist that the body accepts it at any cost?

It is interesting to observe that the scientific and medical worlds are beginning to explore this very question. A television programme (on Channel 4 on Monday 26 June, 2006 in the UK) called *Mindshock: Transplanting Memories* addressed the possibility of the heart having an intellingence of its own including a memory. One person had a bone marrow transplant after which he recorded definite changes in his personality (memories, food preferences, fear, music choices, etc.). Having tracked down the donor family he shared his experiences to find that he had literally taken on the personality of his donor.

A Yale University doctor, found that the heart had a feedback mechanism, a systemic memory, where neurons send out and receive communications. The heart is a hugely energetic organ, always in communication with the brain. Seemingly core central memories continue in the donor heart. A Canadian doctor and research scientist discovered that there is more to the heart than the current model can explain. It is not only a pump, there are neurons outside, and inside the heart where sophisticated connections of neurons exist. It is the brain in the heart that allows it to beat again when transplanted. Some scientists believed that the heart has its own intelligence and possesses a long and short-term memory. If higher memory is stored and transferred in the heart then this must involve the questioning of the ethics involved in transplantation.

It has been noted that immuno-suppressive medications caused mood swings, euphoria, and strange, disturbed thought patterns. Some doctors reluctantly agree that perhaps transplant patients did experience changes in personality, but could not easily make the connection with the organ donation. Naturally, scientists, who rely on hard empiricle facts find it difficult to accept that the feeling heart can contribute to the way we think.

A research study was undertaken by Dr. Rollin McCraty to monitor the responses to stimuli of the heart and the brain. A random selection of people were selected and shown pictures. Some pictures were disturbing, traumatic, joyful etc. The results of this study showed that the heart responded quicker than the brain. As more pictures were shown the heart developed an anticipatory response, which then sent messages to the brain in preparation for body action. These results were clearly demonstrated on monitors.

Scientific discovery of the inner workings of the human body are changing all the time. It was once believed that no bacteria could survive in the stomach because of the hydrochloric acid present. This has been proven wrong by the presence of Helicobacter pylori. If this condition goes untreated it can result in heart disease. Likewise, if gum disease is untreated this too can affect the heart. This seems to suggest that the heart is not an isolated organ but interconnected with, and interdependent on all physiological systems. Dr. Rollin McCraty described the heart as a feeling organ that holds the memory of events and the life lived. If memory exists in other organs within the body, what implications does this have for transplantation in general? What implications does all this have for medicine in the future? What implications does this have for our own decision making? Where is soul consciousness in all this?

In order to perform organ transplantation it is important that the body, whilst it is brain dead, be artificially maintained through blood and air circulation until such time the required organ can be removed. A heart stays alive for up to four hours after being removed and cooled. To all intents and purposes the dead person is kept mechanically alive, and it is reasonable to believe that the soul is then trapped. Some regard this intervention as inappropriate, yet progressive. Are medical people viewing death as a fault, an outrage, and a failure? Does this lead to intrusive medical intervention?

Soul care should be included as part of discussions around care of the dying and choices about the timing of ones own death. Spiritual wellbeing is no less a priority. We seem to identify soul with religious beliefs. Our tradition informs us that care of one's soul irrespective of one's religion is not only a life journey, but a death journey. The problem would seem to be lack of information, and indeed, fear of the unknown.

If we believe that each organ in the body has a living, dynamic life of its own, albeit interconnected with other organs and systems, then when a foreign body, a kidney, heart, or liver, for instance, is introduced it is reasonable to suggest that it would take a long time for the natural organs to relate to the donor. Respect for the dead person is taken away when they are viewed as recyclable material, which reduces the human being to a sum of parts.

I have personally, through meditation and deep contemplation, been allowed to experience what actually happens when the above takes place, otherwise I would not write about it with such passion. I have also been given information from a medical university as to how these transplants occur, and I am not impressed at the disrespect for the living soul and its confused place 'between worlds'.

Sometimes death can be seen as giving up without a fight, and therefore organ donation is giving hope, whilst waiting for an appropriate organ to present itself. This hope grows into despair when a suitable organ is not available, yet the waiting time affords the grieving parents space to deal with their sense of loss. Many will say 'How wonderful the child is given a new life by means of anothers kidney.' This child may live many years with the support of immuno-suppressive drugs, which in actual fact, are potentially carcinogenic. All the time the child and her parents have to be aware of changes taking place as the foreign organ may be rejected by the recipient. This for the dear parents is certainly more acceptable than having to accept the 'premature' death of their child. For that child to have experienced some short years in body life and to have experienced love from parents may be all the soul asked of her this time.

Much support is needed for such parents to view the whole situation from a wider perspective to include soul. We lack this support. When soul education is widely available, and not seen as part of a religious belief system, then people will be able to make conscious, well-informed decisions regarding organ donation for themselves or their children.

Blood transfusions help to maintain life, and are widely used as a healing device in hospitals. It is possible to donate your own blood prior to a surgical procedure therefore negating the need of donor transfusions. According to our Celtic ancestors our story is in the blood. By that we mean our soul's journey travels through the blood circulation whereby we symbolically continue to live and die. The blood in our veins symbolizes the letting go of what no longer serves us, and is transformed into the red, arterial, passionate life-giving blood.

The heart is the Cauldron where everything is stirred into unconditional love. This is the place of filtering, the place of stirring, and the seat of the emotions. Could it be that in giving my blood to another, I am mixing my subtle energies with their subtle energies, and am passing on my unfinished business together with my loves and dislikes? It has been reported that recipients of blood often change personalities or at least experience changes in preferences and values after having received blood transfusions. This I fully understand on an energetic level, and my feeling is that more and more we have to accept that as human beings we are not just blood, sweat, and tears, neither are we just bones, skin, and muscle.

Maybe we have to listen to the wisdom of our ancestors, marry that with advanced medical technology, and then from a place of wisdom including soul, make choices for our lives and our deaths. Medically it is important to have the right blood group matched to your body's needs, but this is only caring for our physiology. What of the whole person? Why not discuss the above with your doctor and friends so that you can explore all sides of this debate. Only then can you come to a conscious decision should you find yourself in the position of having to give or receive an organ or blood

The more we move into the deeper knowledge of the dynamics of energy the more we will understand that life is not dependent on form, nor is formed life at all costs the only reality.

My friend Hannah, who at the moment has metastatic cancer in her kidney, lung, spine, and lymphatic system, says: 'I would not accept a donor organ for many reasons. I truly believe that each cell in my body holds not only my DNA in order for replication to occur, but holds 'memory' of its life in my body, as lived through my experiences. My body is the gift from my soul to experience life, and to try and extend that life artificially is to try and control my soul's journey. Though I am only 50 years old I have no fear of dying, and therefore do not feel the need to extend my life. Doing my grief work now lets me accept the inevitability of death that we all face, the timing of which is not for me to control.'

For me it is important that I donate differently whilst in body life. My question to myself is how do I donate time to others so that their lives may be enriched? For me, it is more difficult to open my heart to some people while alive than to generously donate my organs when I die.

Illness as transition

If we see illness as a way of instruction, of helping us get in touch with the divine then we are actually healing our lives this time. Many people's souls have chosen the route of illness to be a source of enlightenment. Others carry their illness with rage and aggression. Chances for healing are presented to them, but they are not able to see through the mist of their own agony. Many people do not recover their body wellness, but they do experience an immense healing. I have met with many such people, whom I would call great healers. Hannah is one such person. When people can open their hearts to themselves with loving compassion, their experience of illness is transformed. When we come from our heads only, guilt, shame, and even self-hatred are experienced.

Often, the ill person feels responsible for their illness in a way that suggests that it is their 'fault', and the internal conversation can run like this: 'If I had been a more aware person, if I had thought the right thoughts, eaten the right food, lived the right life, had been a better person; if I had been more conscious I would not be dying of cancer right now, and leaving my family to cope.' We must also consider our close encounters with the pollutants in our surroundings and how our neglect of the earth has left us tittering on the edge of annihilation. This is our collective problem, one to which we have all contributed. As long as we stay conscious we can do something about it. The more conscious I become the less physical and energetic pollution I will create.

> 'Self-forgiveness and self-acceptance is something we need to practise during our living moments, so that in our dying moments we can heal into death with joy.'
> — *Hannah Cunningham, Brigit's Day celebration, 2 February 2006.*

Hannah shares more with us:

> 'If I reject my body with all the limitations that cancer is imposing, if I deny my emotions – and there is a multitude of them, if I deny my sexuality – all that makes me feminine, I am not being spiritual, I am being neurotic. So how can I find healing, how can I find wholeness, my holiness if I reject any part of myself?'

> — There will be no growth through struggle – no healing until you put your burdens down.
> — There will be no growth through inner conflict – no healing until you forgive, and are forgiven.
> — There will be no growth – no healing until you live everything.
> — Life is not about struggle.
> — No merit, no growth, and no healing will come from struggle.
> — *Hannah Cunningham 2006*

Language and illness

Language is simply the medium through which we communicate. It gives flesh to ideas, thoughts, and daydreams. The words become flesh and they dwell in us. They are neutral until we give them meaning; but they are loaded with associative recall from past experiences. The Celts used language carefully as it held a power and a potency that could either heal or destroy. Storytelling was their way of recounting today's experience to create tomorrow's history. Words were sacred companions to the bards and Druids, and many words held a magick for priestesses that the ordinary person was not allowed to pronounce or interpret.

It was said that the sea god, *Mannannon McLir,* held a secret magick word on the back of his tongue. When, under duress, he was asked to reveal it, his tongue became a flame of fire that scorched the oppressor. The story of Rapunzel also impresses on us the magick of words, and naming. As a young person, I grew up with the old Irish language fresh in my mouth, and I recall that the word 'soul' and 'name' were pronounced the same. When we name something, we earth it. We imbue it with qualities that the un-named cannot experience. When something is named it is witnessed, it has a right to find expression in life. We need to be careful then about the language we use regarding illness such as cancer. The idea of 'fighting' our cancer is quite unloving and unmerciful. Cancer is seen as the 'enemy': some 'thing' outside our own psyche, against which to wage war, to kill, to annihilate, some 'thing' to fear. Whilst the object of our fear is seen as something over which we have no control, then it will take over and cause havoc.

Abusive language to ourselves leaves us more uneasy and dis-eased. To call the cancer-affected cells in our body, 'invaders', alienates us. If love alone heals, then loving language must be used, if we are to experience true healing. And healing does not necessarily mean body healing alone. Healing includes healing into death.

It is wonderful to know that our nervous systems cannot differentiate between a real experience and an imagined one. Imagination is the stuff of the soul. Visualization affords us the opportunity to transcend everyday so-called reality, and experience the reality of the gods. *Tír na-n-óg* – 'land of the forever young', 'land of milk and honey', 'land over the rainbow' – can be reached through the closing down of our rational minds, and the opening up of that magickal mystery place of creative phenomena. Children know this place. The child in us knows this place. The wonder of the child may seem to have disappeared in many adults, yet when asked to imagine a more creative reality than the one presented to them, they have the ability to rise above given circumstances into an expanded space. In this space, in this Cauldron of plenty, imagination offers herself to us with boundless generosity.

Illness is a time when we need to travel from the given, painful reality into the space of healing. That place where the illness has not touched, and cannot touch. As Hannah would say, this is the place of soul time, that place where divine perfection and absolute healing itself resides, waiting for us to visit, and become acquainted with its healing balm.

It only takes one

When one cell in the body is malfunctioning, the surrounding physiology is influenced negatively. Indeed, cells at a distance may also begin to malfunction; thus the interrelatedness begins between the cells of the body. In the case of cancerous cells, a primary cancer may be detected in a female breast, and soon a secondary or sympathetic malignancy may appear in the uterus. A secondary may be detected first whilst the primary cancer cell may lie dormant. Similarly, cancerous cells may infest a male liver whilst the sympathetic malignancy may show in the prostate. So it appears that in the physiology of the human being, homeostasis depends on peaceful coexistence between the cells of the body.

In the outer physiology, in the greater body of the world, a similarity is observed: a member of the family may contract flu. Soon others will be infected. This may spread to neighbours. So it is also regarding our thought patterns, our thinking in relation to others: if I hold a grudge, revenge, hatred, and refuse to communicate with another body, because of our interrelatedness as human beings I am affecting someone else's thinking somewhere else. I am contributing to dysfunctioning thoughts in another body. The disturbed electromagnetic impulses emanating from me affect other beings in other parts of the world's body. When we realize our interconnectedness with all created phenomena we will realize, hopefully not too late, how the thoughts we hold, the beliefs we manifest have a knock-on effect.

The power of one is mighty because it can manifest illness and well-being. One malfunctioning cell in the body can be responsible for malignancy in other parts of the body. One human being harbouring malignant thoughts can be responsible for malignancy in the body of the world, thus contributing to wars, unrest, so-called fatal accidents. Hatred, quiet rage, preaching a separatist gospel, seeking revenge are all malignant cells in the thought body of humanity. I am responsible for world peace by firstly creating peaceful coexistence with my family. Peace begins at home. Interconnectedness amongst people can achieve global healing that the individual cannot do alone yet begins with the individual. Who was the 'one' in your home who influenced your thinking?

We are all responsible for bringing in the Age of Aquarius with joyful hearts and sharing souls. Water carriers are the ones who having nurtured themselves to go deeper and deeper into the world and help to quench the thirst of others. We are entering into a difficult time for the cosmos; as within, so without. Maybe it is not too late to hold back the streams of fear that create war.

A self-healing visualization

— *Sit or lie down, whichever is more comfortable. With your eyes closed, get in touch with your breath. Be aware of breathing in, and breathing out: every in breath an invitation to life; every out breath an invitation to die. Breathe thus for the next five breaths.*

— *Imagine the part of your body that is calling out for your love in this moment. See it as a vulnerable, unloved child needing reassurance that he/she is loved. With your right hand, cradle this part of your body, and with your breath send warm, loving kindness and mercy to this needy child. Keep focusing on your breath.*

— *Keep in touch with the child. Let the breath bring your attention to any pain you may be experiencing in this moment. With the next in breath, imagine that your whole heart is opening out to divine love and mercy, filling your lungs completely with this healing balm. Now direct the out breath to where your hand is, the place that needs your love, and the place that needs divine mercy.*

— *Keep breathing thus until you become distracted, and when you do, open your eyes. Keep your hand on your body and after a moment, close your eyes again, and go back to the practice. Every time you get distracted, do not worry — no condemnation, just open your eyes, and when you are ready, continue the practice.*

Forgiveness of ourselves is essential to healing. This following exercise has been the source of much healing to people living and healing with cancer:

— *Now gently hear these words coming through your breath to your body: 'Forgive me I did not see you. Forgive me I did not hear your pain. Forgive me I did not feel your fear. Forgive me I did not acknowledge your vulnerability. Forgive me I did not honour your journey. Forgive me I did not grieve your losses.'*

— *Next in breath, breathe in healing, loving energy, directing this energy again to your body, using the words: 'I see you. I hear your pain. I feel your fear. I acknowledge your vulnerability. I honour your journey. I grieve your loss.'*

— *Having repeated the above for the third time, remain in silence. Feel the warmth of your hand cradling your body, as you would a child who is ill. When you are ready, open your eyes. Do not move for a while, but take in the whole of your environment through your senses.*

Dialoguing with cancer

If your body has just taken on cancer (maybe to help you become more aware of your emotional hurts), then ask a friend or speak into a tape the following exercise:

Sit in a chair, or lie on your bed. Be comfortable and breathe easily. Become aware of the part of your body that holds the cancer in this moment.

Find an image, be with the image, and say to the image: 'I understand at a head level that you are a messenger to me. I understand at head level that you have something important to say to me about my life, and about my death. I am afraid of you. You scare me. You could be the means of my death. I do not want to have to look at you. I do no want to listen to you. At a head level, you are my enemy. I hate you. I want to kill you. I want to be rid of you. I want to live as long as possible, without having to think of death.' You can add any other accusations that come to you.

Now feel all this at a deep level. Feel your truth in it. Feel what it's like to look in the face of your so-called executioner. Do not deny any of your feelings. Feel them and name them out loud. Breathe deeply. Maintain comfort in your body for the next five breaths.

Now open your eyes. Look around you, stretch your arms, and ask your own guides and angel beings to help you. Ask them to sit with you and give you their help and guidance.

Now sit in a chair opposite. Close your eyes. You are the symbol for cancer. Feel what that is like. Feel what it is like to be hated. Feel what it is like to be the source of such grief and misery. Feel what it is like to have such power. Stay in this place until the symbol changes, and when it does, submit this symbol to paper using crayons.

Now go back to the other chair. With your eyes open, take on the energy of one of your wise guides, and listen to what they have to say. You are a wise guide ready to help, and give your considered advice to this person in the other chair, namely you. Allow this guide to tell you everything about your illness – why you have it, and the message it brings. This wise guide knows exactly why you have contracted this illness, and why it is important that you hear what it has to say. Listen in silence as your guide speaks from the other chair. Later on, write down everything you heard.

Healing art

Since cave men days, art has been a way of representing the environment, a way of representing the inner pastures, the unconscious. Language alone cannot, and is not meant to delve into the deeper caves of our consciousness. It is too dependent on the intellect as sole knower. The soul speaks to us, even sings to us through colour and symbol, and is a reliable source of that knowledge that is unapproachable through reason. This is why I use art as a wonderful guide and helpmate in the healing process. I have problems when the so-called therapist interprets the art of another because the artist herself is the true interpreter, and we simply have to know the right questions to ask. Here is an example of what I mean. Again, ask a friend to witness the exercise with you:

— *Find crayons and paper and sit comfortably. Close your eyes and get in touch with the disease of your body. Breathe in and out slowly. Find a symbol or colour that represents it. Get a heart-full sense of it so that you could reproduce it quite easily.*

— *Open your eyes and represent the symbol on paper, using all the colours available. Write on the paper any feelings you have about it. Become aware of the colours you used, and what they have to say.*

— *Now begin to ask questions. What are you? Why are you here? What do you need from me? What are you a reminder of? What is it I would not have heard had you not come? How can you help me? Write down everything. Leave out nothing, no matter how grotesque, or meaningless it may seem.*

— *Now listen.*

— *When you have completed this exercise give thanks, and close your eyes. Let the breath take you deeper as you get in touch with the affected part of your body, and with your two hands cradling your body's pain, speak words of love, and non-condemnation of the sweetest mercy and heart-felt compassion for this part of you that has made room for this messenger in your life. This part of your body has sacrificed itself for you. Become aware of the grief, because pain carries bgrief, and your body is experiencing pain. The more you can truly believe that all illness is about loss, is about grieving, then the more you will direct your compassion to it, and see it as you would a bereaved person.*

My friend Hannah said to me today, 'When someone grieves the loss of another, it is clear, the person has left either in death or has gone away. While you feel the deep sense of loss and grief, it is ultimately outside yourself. When grieving an illness, or possible terminal illness, the grief is connected with an ever-changing bodily state that goes with you hourly, daily. There is no escape. I often feel immersed in deep grief that has no words or other expression, and when that time passes, when it has been embraced, acceptance floods in again. This continuum of grief and acceptance is mostly an isolated experience for us all I guess.'

This isolated experience that Hannah speaks of is the knowing that no matter what help may come from outside, essentially conscious aloneness, conscious willingness, and conscious creativity can transform. The alchemist, the alchemy, and the gold, lie within the human psyche. This creative being invites the outer to come and sit at the hearth of her own longing, and lovingly watch as she moulds and shapes the lead of her pain, into the gold of pure consciousness.

One of the greatest transformations in nature is a metamorphosis of a caterpillar into a butterfly. The caterpillar dissolves its earth material. If this dissolution does not happen a colourful butterfly cannot emerge. If the caterpillar resists this transitionary stage, the stage where nothing seems to be happening, this space between breaths where movement is curtailed, the place of surrender, the silent space where miracles are birthed, then the metamorphosis struggles to produce new life. We humans, unfortunately, resist this space, this space of seeming non-movement, of stillness, often called depression and lethargy, and for many seen as annihilation. And yet, it is the annihilation of our limitations only.

Internal landscapes *(Tirdhreach istigh)*

The creativity of the Celts expressed itself in many ways, especially in the intricate art in the stonework of burial and ritual spaces. In New Grange in Ireland, the stone that stands outside the entrance to the burial chamber is well known, and draws tourists from all parts of the world. Many have tried to interpret the symbols, but who can truly know the mind of a culture over 2,500 years old. We are like children trying to study physics. For me the intricacy of my own internal landscape and ritual spaces is a study, a mystery, a wonder, and a humbling, yet enlightening discovery. Much more awe-full than any standing stone or piece of Celtic artistry. This discovering of my own ancient sites (sights) through the passageways, through the caves of my own darkness, my own burial grounds, is what I am excavating. This I do not do with spades and chisels, but with the stuff of my own healing. I am honoured to be allowed to call on the help of such wonderful, creative resources as my Celtic ancestors to point out, to show, to explore the riches of the unfathomable wealth of my own soul's ancient past and present consciousness.

Concsciousness meditations

This inner landscape we talk about is that rich soil, which holds the ancient imprint of all natural phenomena; in other words it is the sacred place that holds the imprint or the DNA of all my evolutionary stages from invertebrate to human. Soul in us is the carrier of all my evolutionary imprints. She holds the impressions, which I have lived and earthed. Relying on this truth I introduce you to this meditation, which, when performed at the right time in your own consciousness development, can and does bring you forward into a place of non-duality, oneness with all, and a sense of healing even though you may be on your deathbed.

— *If possible be in the open air with nature, either at the seaside, in the mountains, or in a forest. If it is not possible to be in the open air, imagine a time you were. Be alone. Find a place to sit down and become aware of your breath, consciously slowing it down.*

— *Become aware of your environment. If you are at the sea for example be mindful of the waters in front of you, of the waves crashing onto the shore. It is important during these visualizations that you have a sensory experience only, not a cognitive one. Our sensory experience shows us simply sea, flower, mountain, without evaluation as if we are seeing it for the first time, without our conditioned projections. This gives us mindfulness without preconceived ideas so we see pure instead of tainted image.*

— *Breathe, and as you do, breathe in the sea. Breathe it into the water in your own being. Imagine as you breathe in the sea the water in your own body dissolves into it, so much so that you become totally immersed in the waters in front of you, that you merge with other seas and oceans until at last your own being is no longer separate from the being of ocean. There are no longer two beings; there is one being, and that is water.*

— *The pain in your body is also immersed in this great ocean so much so that it is no longer your pain, it is the ocean's pain, it is the pain; and as oceans merge into each other the pain becomes dissolved until there is only water flowing. Stay with this awareness as you gaze deeply into the sea in front of you, breathing with the waves. You are present and aware yet the you that carried the pain has gone, and the pain has been dissolved. Now there is only beingness; and that beingness is simply the breath, not your breath, not the waves breath, but breath. Breath is life, breath is spirit, and we are one.*

— *When you are ready, close your eyes, and from a place of gratitude for the element of water, breathe deeply and smile.*

Use the same format as above when you bring forest and mountain into your consciousness. It is a great gift to offer a dying person the facility of being at the ocean, in a forest, or near mountains, and help them experience these healing meditations. The length of time one stays in each meditation depends on the energy of the dying person. Nevertheless one does not have to be dying in the body in order to gain full benefit from these visualizations. Try them and see.

Chapter 12

Gathered In

Heavy metal healing
- Thank you Slayer

Another wonderful story I would like to share is the story of Steffen who was just 23 years old, and was dying with a malignant inoperable brain tumour. He had had many operations but the cancer could not be arrested. He had difficulty speaking because the left side of his face was paralyzed. He had a younger brother called Paschal, who was 13 years old. Their mother wept long tears on my shoulder about her Steffen and I understood every tear. Steffen had mentioned suicide a few times to his physiotherapist, Annette, and she was worried about this.

As I took in the different artifacts in Steffen's bedroom I got an intuitive feel about it all. I looked across at this big man, only 23 years old, in a wheelchair, no hair, the many scars of operations visible on his head, new black leather bovver boots unlaced (that was the fashion), all dressed in black with 'Slayer' printed boldly and fiercely across his t-shirt. He was obviously a heavy metal fan. I noticed two steel guitars in the corner and some CDs on the shelf along with a soft, fluffy bunny rabbit. For those of you who are not acquainted with heavy metal, they are aggressive in their musical content and looks, far from the soft, fluffy bunny – and maybe not! With an invitation from Steffen I sat facing him.

'I'm thinking, Steffen, it must be terrible to be in this wheelchair and not be able to walk around.'

'It is, Phyllida.' he answered and kept his eyes on me.

'You have never been able to walk in your new boots, eh?'

'No.'

'That must be tough.'

'Yeah, tough.'

'I see you like Slayer.'

'Yeah, and I like the lyrics.'

'My son was into heavy metal, too, and I recognize the pictures.'

'I met them once in Hamburg, they were great and I got pictures taken with them.'

'Can I see them?'

Steffen beckoned to Annette to take down the box behind her on the shelf, and he showed us the photographs of himself taken with the band. This brought a great smile to his sad face.

'I see, Steffen, that you had long hair then, two years ago.'

'Yeah, Phyllida, I had to get it all cut off when I had the operations.'

'That must have been really sad for you, eh?'

'Yeah, I liked my long hair, but I have it in a box over there.' Again Annette brought the box out of which came Steffen's lovely long golden locks, all in tact. With an obvious tear in his eye he said 'It is all here now.' as he closed the box with his poor disfigured hands.

'I see you played the guitar, Steffen.'

'Yeah, I liked to play heavy metal, but this flat was too small.' He lived in a block of flats.

'It must be awful not to be able to play your guitar, Steffen.'

'Yeah, not so good Phyllida.'

'Heavy metal has a lot of drum sound, yeah?'

'Yeah, I love the drums, but they are too loud for here, and too expensive.'

I had got it! I knew why I was there and I was excited. 'I can give a concert and get money for the drums... and we will get a place for you to go a few times a week to play your CDs and play your drums.'

Steffen had his head bent in his chest, and did not look up. I knew he had heard me, and he needed time to take it all in. At last he said: 'that would be good, Phyllida that would be good.'

Tears dimmed his eyes when I suggested that the family could get together and sew his hair to a band so that when he played he could also wear his own hair. Heavy metal musicians like to have the hair all around their face as they perform. The family was delighted, and the day came for the concert and they were all there. Steffen played his drums, which Annette had bought in the meantime. People came from all around to support the event, the highlight of which was Steffen playing the drums. During the concert Steffen lit a yellow candle for Patrick, who was dying in Northern Ireland from a brain tumour also. I visited Steffen many times after this, and I realized the joy that day had brought him and his whole family. They had so many photographs to look at with fond memories. It gave them all a chance to share their grief and their joy, and it bonded the community together in a way that was very intimate. There was a couple at the concert, whose baby had died some years before, and they could weep again together for their child. The event had healed something in them too.

On the evening before he died I knew Steffen had done what he needed to do this time round. His dream of playing drums in public was so precious to him, and the photographs are living proof that dreams can come true even before we die. Much to my surprise, Steffen had requested I sing 'Amazing Grace' with an up-tempo beat at his funeral. He was also dressed in his Slayer t-shirt, and I put the CD into the coffin to accompany him. Steffen had his form of a happy death.

Paschal went through a difficult time when his big brother was ill. He did so much for Steffen amidst his own deep grief and confusion. It is really difficult for parents to have to deal with all the family feelings and often there is little help given to the siblings, who need a lot of attention. After all they are not dying, so they are expected to be grateful. Paschal was involved in the care of his brother up until the end.

Young children and death

The following are excerpts from a workshop I gave in 1990.

Young children absorb their environment, the feelings, ideas, beliefs, and non-verbal communication of the adults around them. It is natural that they do so. This is the way cultures survive and continue. What we teach young children, or what young children absorb contributes to their psychological and behavioural patterns. No doubt what a child learns from the parent, especially the mother, and teacher at school, whether verbal or non-verbal, affects them in one way or another. Therefore, messages about death, God, love, feelings, leave important imprints, often forming part of their thinking processes about life and death.

If a young child is told that his brother has died because God wanted him for an angel, the child sees God as a thief, the taker of life. When I was a Montessori teacher in the 80s, one child told me quite boldly: 'God is a big bully. He steals people.' Another child maintained: 'God is a big body snatcher.' God was always referred to as He, masculine and big, therefore, powerful. We forget that a child sees things literally. Their minds view abstract concepts in picture images they already know. They have their own symbolic translations for events and traumas. For instance, when we tell a child: 'Daddy has gone to heaven to God's home, and he is very happy there.' then the child believes that daddy left them and went to God's home because he did not like their home and was not happy with them.

A young child was told one day: 'Stop crying or mummy will go away.' As it happened the mother in question died of a sudden heart attack, three days later, and the child believed that she was the cause of her death. When we tell a child, for example, that God wanted your little baby sister because she was very special, the child believes himself not to be special, and so views God with much anger and frustration. Such a child can grow up 'very good', so as to obtain specialness. God as the taker of life has all the power, and the child has no redress, no comeback, nowhere to direct her hurt, anger, loss, and sense of unfairness. If she sees her parents bravely carrying the grief, not protesting, not openly crying their pain because death is seen as God's will, then the child shuts up, learns to bravely carry the grief, and sees this as the right way to suffer loss. God's will must not be questioned.

Conversely, when a child sees a parent crying, expressing their sadness the child tries to 'make things better' by refraining from mentioning the loss, thus carries her grief inactively. Thus, it is important for families to share grief together. In our Western culture the idea of having young children round the deathbed of a father/mother or sibling is still not the norm. We keep death quiet, secret, and usually for hospitals. Children are not included in the rituals. They are sent away to protect them from grieving adults. If children are excluded from the death ceremonies, they are also excluded from the healing processes within the family. Children know innately how to grieve loss. Observe a young child whose toy is snatched from her. She screams: 'Give me back my toy.' or 'Mine, mine, mine.' She gets angry; she will bargain with you sometimes: 'I will be good if you give me back my toy.' She gets moody if she does not get it back, and she eventually finds something else to amuse her. But she will have her natural feelings first until she learns that 'nice girls don't cry or scream', and 'it is not OK to be angry'.

When we do not allow a child to grieve naturally, we teach them to suppress feelings, to disbelieve their own innate need to cry, but to swallow the hurt, to always defer to another's way of dealing with pain, and to distrust their own inner authority in the form of natural responses to hurt and loss.

Long ago in Ireland, children were always present at wakes and funerals. They cried their tears with the neighbours and their children when they came to offer sympathy. They stayed at the deathbed whilst a parent breathed their last breath. Often the youngest child in the family was the one to place the rosary beads in the hands of a dying parent, or a grandmother/grandfather. Many an adult recalls having been on the bed of a dying parent as a child; watching and concentrating as they departed this life, and naturally went onto the next life.

I recall one small child saying to me: 'Mummy died and her eyes were open, and daddy closed them, and then she could sleep.' Death is no stranger to these children. They see death as the natural progression of life/death transition. They speak of the life in the next life with ease and objectivity. Death holds no sting or dread. They were not excluded from its visitations as young children (neither do they view birth as something reserved for doctors and nurses). They were trained up in the way of living and dying, and when old did not have to depart from it.

Children use symbolic language when trying to explain to the adult mind what they are going through. One such way is through the medium of art and drawings. In this way, the unconscious mind reveals itself. If we as adults have eyes to see the messages, and ears to hear the messages, we will understand what the young person is trying to convey, in a way that language cannot do. Carl G. Jung and other great souls have left us interesting insights regarding the interpretation of art and children. Greg Firth, an American, whom I had the privilege of working with in Virginia, has researched many pieces of children's drawings, and used the same for interpretations of childhood dysfunctioning. My own work with psycho drawing has been a great help to me and others.

When working with clients in a therapeutic way going through issues of loss and abuse they leave their mark on a page; they leave part of their story, and not just what the physical eye can see. Two children were asked to draw 'death' as an exercise sometime after the death of a family member. One child drew a circle of black, and the other drew a sunset/sunrise of blazing orange and yellow. It was interesting to hear the children's views and their own interpretations of their drawings. One child saw death as a 'Big black hole.' and when I asked what is in the hole, he replied 'Monsters if you are bad.' And if you are good I asked, 'I suppose God.' was the reply. The other child answered, 'It is the sun rising and setting.' And to the question, tell me about it, she continued 'When you die it is the sun setting, and when you are born it is the sun rising.' I never forgot what I learned about death from children. Children are our teachers. (I suggest *The Snowman*[xiv] as a marvellous book for children to learn about letting go, and grief.)

A DANCE OF WHOLENESS
Then I shall dance, a dance of wholeness
Straight to the heart of Love.
The dream times between breaths are shorter now
As soul memory wipes the sad mist
From our swollen eyes
To reveal our fingerprints yours and mine
Moist
Round the cup of our becoming.
Next time I'll choose a gentler landing place
Where warm, soft grass
Will cradle my fall from grace
And softer too,
The arms my weaning will embrace
And glad, glad songs
Will lullaby my innocence…
— *P. Anam-Áire, 1991*

Seá.

Pronunciation of Gaelic Words and Expressions

an athair	an ahar
anam úilioch	anam ill-ee-och
an cailleach	an kail-yach
an Eolath	an yolach
an maighdean	an myd-chen
an mathair	an mach-ar
an óige	an oy-gih
ag leanbh-áire	egg lanv-ayre
aite	atcha
an duach	an dooach
aonacht	eanacht
bean céile	ban Kayla
beatha	ba-ha
céile	kay-le
claddagh	kladda
cú cuchlainn	ku kulanns
duine aoifa	dinna eefa
dul amach	dul amach
Fionn MacCumhaill	Finn Mack-Kuhill
láimhe céile	lava kayla
lé chéile	leh kayla
mat hair mór	ma har more
marbh tráthúil	marv trah-hool
ordú nádúrtha	ordu nadurha
Queen Meadhbh	Queen Meev
scéalta	skayl-tah
seabhéans	shavans
tír na-n-óg	cheer na n-og
Tírdhreach ishtigh	cheer-dra istee
tuatha de Dannan	thu-ha de Dannan

The Celts

They came from Russia in the third millennium BC, and were known as a passionate, earthy tribe of people. They studied mathematics, astrology, and the sleep of the dead. Three tribes settled in Asia Minor, where they founded the town of Ankara, (*anam cara* –'soul friend'), and it was later named Galatia. The Gundestrop Cauldron was found in a Danish bog in Gundestrop, and depicts the prestige of Celtic art. It is interesting to note the horned god, *Cerunnos*, in a half-lotus position, holding a Celtic torc in his right hand, whist in his left hand he holds the serpent (100 BC). The torc represents the cycle of life, death, and life, and the serpent represents the kundalini energy of life force.

On *Cerunnos'* head are the antlers of the stag, seven branches on each antler, which could depict the seven energy centres of the body. A stag stands beside him. This Buddhic posture, one of meditation and centredness, is attributed to a Celtic god, thus we see the influence of Indo-European culture in Celtic history. The Celts refused to keep records, and resisted being dragged into the boring continuum of history, and held to dreamtime, the eternal now. Oral tradition, therefore, and the telling of stories, and the trimmings of the stories is a great gift from our Celtic ancestors.

I have tried to reach an intuitive understanding of contemporary Celtic Consciousness by remembering the mythology, *scéalta* or 'stories' handed down to us from generation to generation. Most of these stories I would have learned and heard through the medium of Gaelic or Irish, and no doubt the Irish love to tell the story and add their own bit to it! It is however clear that the Celts believed that life itself has a certain rhythm or cycle and that all creation has its own life span and movement. One full cycle of breath took millions of years, and so the great breath is still creating its evolutionary creation on the earth, and in all other worlds, seen and unseen.

The Irish are a very romantic people and it would seem that we have inherited this heart-involvement with life from our Celtic origins. We love the use of vivid imagination to include poetry and drama. The drama of dying is something my particular ancestors wrote about in poetry and story. My father's father's use of language was dramatic, sensuous, and poignant. The Celtic soul is steeped in symbolism and living the symbolic life adds both colour and dynamism to the most mundane situation. For this I am grateful because nothing is as it appears in the mind of the Celt but in the very bloodstream of nature herself are such mystories and magick making. Living the elemental life brings us closer to our primal nature, soul.

It was believed that the soul could be liberated by fire and air; and Brigit held that as the earth body flamed to the sky, so the soul released herself in all the colours ranging from red earth, through orange, and yellow, through to turquoise, purple, and white. The smoke being the offering to spirit of an earthed expression of itself joining breath again. A consciousness of death was always present, just beyond perception, secretly guiding human actions, and giving richness to rituals. The rhythms and pulsatings of nature became the patterns of the metres of poetry the Celtic bards relied on. They breathed poetry, whilst in trance, to instil in the memory the visions they had encountered.

The Celts also studied herbs and they taught that the land was a living entity, aware of, and responsive to humans. They had to bow to its inhumane nature and requirements, as nature was the ultimate reality to which all must eventually bow. Personalized earth manifests herself with goddess/nature, whose favour had to be won. Kinship was the only social cement in the Celtic world. One's only unquestionable allegiance was to nature and one's family, and the tribe was a vast extended family. Children were adopted by non-blood relations so that they could learn the gifts and the creativity from different backgrounds. They have shown us a way not to revert to barbarous living conditions, but to a rich soulfulness without which no individual, no family, no tribe, no nation can expand consciously.

Summary of Christian
and Celtic beliefs

Christian beliefs

- Original sin – here to suffer, expect to suffer
- Heaven as a reward – hell as punishment-both without the self
- Children of Adam need to be redeemed – saviour/rescuer needed
- Eve, archetypal feminine – temptress, disobedient
- Man has dominion over all creation
- God is our father in heaven – child relationship
- Good and bad, emphasis on polarization
- Personality and gender attributed to God - God is male,wrathful, angry, jealous
- Human beings responsible for death of God's son – guilt and shameas consequences
- God must be feared/loved – contradiction
- Body is seen as unworthy – subjugation of women
- Gospel of good works – love others first
- Patriarchal language – hell, torture, commandments, punishment, demands
- Certain days set aside for holiness – Sundays and holy days
- Death is seen as end of life – one try at salvation
- Consciousness of the patriarchy
- Humility is about hating the self and this is good
- Need for repentance because of our guilt
- Faith is an intellectual journey
- Time set apart for prayer and meditation
- Ego is our innate evil, which must be destroyed

Summary of Christian and Celtic beliefs

Celtic beliefs

- Original mystery – suffering seen as over-identification
- We come from love – here to ground the divine
- Not a reward/punishment philosophy
- When we are soulfully led we do not need external saviours
- Soul is the archetypal 'Eve' delighting in her earthedness
- Nature is our guide and mentor
- Responsible for one's own life here, and hereafter
- Non-polarization of good and bad – integration of dark/light, death/life etc.
- Genderless life force that keeps everything in motion
- We are not responsible for the death of Jesus the Christ
- Pure love casts out all fear
- Enlightenment attained through process of incarnation.
- The trinity includes so-called masculine and feminine energies
- Everything is part of the holiness of life – we do not become holy, we *are* holy
- Death is seen as a pause in a series of lives, many chances to heal
- Language is soul language – everything has symbolic representation
- Humility is knowing who I am without false declaration
- Faith is a soul-led journey without emphasis on destination
- Prayer is an integral part of everyday blessing
- Self-compassion is the beginning of healing
- Earth-mind is not a force to be destroyed but loved into wholeness
- Everything is in-formation for me about my life.

Endnotes

i   Louise B.Young, *The Unfinished Universe*,
      (New York: Oxford University Press, 1983).

ii   Phyllida Anam-Áire, *Love Beyond Understanding* , CD, 2005.

iii   Phyllida Anam-Áire, *Let Love In,* CD, 2000.

iv   Phyllida and Healing Voices, *Touched,* CD, 2003.

v   Phyllida Anam-Áire, *A Celtic Book of Dying,*
      (Findhorn Scotland: Findhorn Press, 2005).

vi   Phyllida Anam-Áire and Healing Voices, *Touched,* CD, 2003.

vii   Phyllida Anam-Áire and Healing Voices, *Touched,* CD, 2003.

viii   Phyllida Anam-Áire and Healing Voices, *Touched,* CD, 2003.

ix   Phyllida Anam-Áire, *Love Beyond Understanding,* CD, 2005.

x   Phyllida Anam-Áire, *Love Beyond Understanding,* CD, 2005.

xi   Phyllida Anam-Áire, *Love Beyond Understanding,* CD, 2005.

xii   Phyllida Anam-Áire, *Love Beyond Understanding,* CD, 2005.

xiii   Phyllida Anam-Áire, *A Celtic Book of Dying,*
      (Findhorn Scotland: Findhorn Press, 2005).

xiv   Raymond Briggs, *The Snowman,*
      (London: Penguin Books Ltd.), 1989.

A Celtic Book of Dying

Watching with the Dying, Travelling with the Dead

BY

PHYLLIDA ANAM-ÁIRE

The Celts believed in the transmigration of the soul, in the magical rhythm of life with a particular order of coming and going for each soul. As they celebrated every new stage of their lives with a ritual they also honoured the passing on of a soul – the death of the physical body: embedded in the natural order of things, women, the facilitators of birth and death, used to care for the dying, easing their transition from this world into the next.

160 pages paperback – ISBN 978-1-84409-048-8

Books, Card Sets,
CDs & DVDs
that inspire and uplift

For a complete catalogue,
please contact:

Findhorn Press Ltd
305a The Park, Findhorn
Forres IV36 3TE
Scotland, UK

Telephone
+44-1309-690582
Fax
+44-1309-690036
eMail
info@findhornpress.com

or consult our catalogue online
(with secure order facility) on
www.findhornpress.com